WRITTEN in BLOOD

WRITTEN IN BLOOD

a brief history of civilisation
(with all the gory bits left in)

BEVERLEY MACDONALD

CARTOONS BY **ANDREW WELDON**

ALLEN&UNWIN

First published in 2003

Allen & Unwin
83 Alexander St
Crows Nest NSW 2065
Australia
Phone: (61 2) 8425 0100
Fax: (61 2) 9906 2218
Email: info@allenandunwin.com
Web: www.allenandunwin.com

Distributed in the UK, Eire and Europe by
Frances Lincoln Ltd., London NW5 2RZ

National Library of Australia
Cataloguing-in-Publication entry:
MacDonald, Beverley.
Written in blood: a brief history of civilisation (with all the gory bits left in).
Includes index.
For teenagers.
ISBN 1 86508 792 0.
1. History – Juvenile literature. I. Weldon, Andrew, 1971– . II. Title.
909

Cover and text design by Sandra Nobes
Set in 12 pt Rotis Serif by TouCan Design
Printed in Australia by McPherson's Printing Group

10 9 8 7 6 5 4 3 2

*This book is for my dad, E.W. (Bill) Smith,
and for the hundreds of students he taught during his
long career at Kensington Primary School, Pakenham
Upper P.S., Myrtleford Consolidated, Mildura P.S.,
Morwell (Tobruk St) P.S., Nar Nar Goon P.S.,
Corryong Consolidated, Murtoa P.S., Rye P.S.,
and Hallam P.S.*

*Once again, many thanks to my brother Chris
for his brilliant last-minute research.*

contents

A FIRST WORD

I can still remember sitting up the back of a dusty classroom, wishing I was anywhere but there. History was boring, just endless names and dates and places that no longer existed. How could dead people possibly be relevant to my life?

I did like to read, though, and I chanced across two novels by Robert Graves set in ancient Rome, *I, Claudius* and *Claudius the God*. I devoured them under the bedcovers at night, captivated

BEVERLEY! PUT DOWN THAT BOOK! HOW ARE YOU EVER GOING TO **LEARN** ANYTHING IF YOU'RE ALWAYS **READING?!**

by the lurid story of how Claudius – the fool, the cripple, the stutterer – survived his murderous family's long tradition of killing off rivals to the imperial throne. Some of Claudius's relatives were sentenced to death and executed, others were poisoned or forced to commit suicide, while others were bricked into a room and starved to death. But everyone ignored Claudius because they thought he was stupid and no real threat. Instead, he outlived them all and was finally proclaimed Emperor.

Alas, Claudius could not escape his fate forever, and eventually his fourth wife fed him a dish of poisoned mushrooms so her son, Nero, could inherit the throne.

By the time I'd finished reading about Claudius, I was hooked. History stopped being dates and names and became stories instead: stories of people who behaved remarkably like people do today.

There was the story of Crassus, the richest man in Rome, who gave a new meaning to the expression 'fire sale'. Whenever there was a fire in the narrow streets of the overcrowded city, Crassus would rush to the scene and start haggling with the distraught landlord. Only when Crassus had bought the burning building at a bargain price would he order his slaves to help extinguish the blaze. Few landlords refused, and Crassus just got richer and richer.

Or the story of Claudius's uncle, the emperor Tiberius, who withdrew from public life to the beautiful Isle of Capri, where he pursued a very strange lifestyle and grew more and more paranoid. Tiberius did not like visitors to drop in unannounced, and when a poor fisherman scaled the cliffs to present the emperor with a freshly caught mullet, Tiberius ordered his guards to rub the fish in the man's face before they threw him back over the cliff into the sea. Or so the story goes...

People don't really change. We are still motivated by greed and lust, envy and pride, fear and anger, as well as love and friendship, loyalty, mercy, courage and compassion. So how does human society ever change? Throughout history some people have been inspired to ask the big questions: Where did we come from? Why are we here? Why do we live like this? Is this the right way to treat each other, or is there a better way?

Suddenly I understood how dead people were relevant to my life. Times are changing, and will continue to change, and history is the story of those changes. There is no slavery in Australia today, but there was slavery in ancient Rome. Instead of the murderous traditions of dysfunctional imperial Roman families, modern democratic governments are decided by elections. Guilt and innocence are decided in courts of law. And fires are extinguished by community-funded fire brigades rather than by unscrupulous individuals looking to make a quick profit.

Who we are now, what we believe in, and how we behave, are forever influenced by what has happened before – by history. And the history of human civilisation is written in blood...

GETTING

CIVILISED

uncivilised civilisation

What makes people civilised? When do we judge that this or that group of people has created a civilisation? Do they mean the same thing? To be civil is to conform to normal standards of politeness. To civilise is to adopt laws and order, and encourage the arts and science; it also means to refine taste and manners. A civilisation is a community that can meet all these requirements.

Some historians would disagree with this definition, defining the moment when people triumph over their environment and reshape it to suit themselves as the first mark of civilisation. Build cities and roads and temples, and you're on your way to civilisation. But is a civilisation necessary civilised?

Many ancient cultures practised human sacrifice to appease their gods, believing that throwing a few maidens or young men into the crater might quieten a volcano god. Other cultures were quite comfortable with ritual cannibalism, while others were utterly dependent on slavery. Today we would consider such practices uncivilised, but it wasn't always so.

cannibalism

There is archaeological evidence that prehistoric Neanderthals practised cannibalism: Neanderthal bones have been found with 'cutting' marks similar to those on animal bones slaughtered and cut up for food. Similar evidence has been found in many cultures – the ancient Aztecs ate the bodies of human sacrifices, New Guinea tribespeople killed and ate captives, and some Native Americans cremated their dead and ate the ashes afterwards.

Why do people eat each other? There are several answers. The most obvious is food: societies that are short of animal protein might take the opportunity to eat meat, and some cannibalism in New Guinea was for just that reason. The Native Americans consumed the ashes of their dead as a mark of respect, while the Aztecs probably practised 'sacred' cannibalism, and ate the bodies of human sacrifices as part of a magical ritual that would bring them closer to their gods.

Other ritual cannibalism hoped to transfer the traits of the dead person to the living through 'sympathetic magic': eating a brave warrior's heart could help make you brave. In the eighteenth century, a Chinese emperor was so impressed with the courage of a defeated Vietnamese woman general, he ordered her to be trampled to death by elephants, and her heart, arms, liver and lungs to then be fed to his troops so that her fierce spirit might be passed on to them. As late as the 1960s, a tribe of native people living in the Amazon practised two quite distinct types of cannibalism. The Wari tribe ate their defeated enemies as a mark of anger and disdain, but they ate the bodies of their loved ones who had died out of affection and respect.

Famine and Cannibalism

From 1315 to 1317, Europe was in the grip of a terrible famine. The weather had been extremely cold, the crops had failed for several years in a row so there was almost nothing to eat, and people were dying in huge numbers. In Ireland, fresh bodies were dug up from their graves and eaten, while executed criminals were consumed in Silesia. Widespread cannibalism was reported from Britain to the Baltic, as people became desperate enough to eat the dead (and there were plenty of them).

This happened again during the late sixteenth century when temperatures plunged during the 'Little Ice Age'. The Thames River in London froze over several times, and at Marseilles, France in 1564, it was so cold that even the sea froze. For four successive years the crops failed. People ate cats and dogs, and once again practised cannibalism. In fact, the weather didn't really improve until the mid-nineteenth century. Scientists have studied the growth patterns of tree trunks and ice samples deep in the Arctic and Antarctic ice, and have calculated that the temperature in the late 1500s was only about 1°C colder that it is today. It doesn't sound like much, but it was enough to shorten the growing season by about a month and lower the altitude at which crops could be grown.

After the Russian revolution, government policy drove many farmers from the land, and a drought in 1921 led to mass starvation. A visiting English Quaker described the scene in one village:

> 'There are practically no babies and those that survive look ghastly. The mothers have no milk and pray that death may come quickly. Slow starvation is too painful ... According to government figures, ninety percent of the children between the ages of one and three have already died from the famine.'

Once again the people ate cats, dogs and horses and resorted to cannibalism.

SO THE STORY GOES ...
IS IT MURDER?

One of the most famous murder trials in English law involved cannibalism. In 1884, a fifty-foot yacht, the *Mignonette*, set sail from England to Australia with the captain, Tom Dudley, and a crew of three on board. Things went well at first, but after they crossed the equator they encountered heavy weather, and on 3 July a huge wave broke over the yacht and the *Mignonette* began to sink. The captain ordered the crew to abandon the ship and, with only moments to spare, they jumped into the dinghy with six cans of food and a cask of water. In the ensuing struggle they lost the cask of fresh water and all but one of the cans.

They patched up the dinghy as best they could, and beat off a large shark during the first night. At one stage they managed to catch a turtle and eat it, and they did trap a little rainwater, but with no stored water and only one can of parsnips, their situation was perilous. The cabin boy was so thirsty he drank sea water, and after nearly three weeks he was critically sick and delirious. The captain brought up the topic they had all been avoiding: in order to survive they were going to have to eat someone, and the dying cabin boy looked like the best prospect. On the nineteenth day, Tom Dudley cut the cabin boy's throat with a penknife and they drank his blood and ate parts of his body.

Four days later, a German ship miraculously appeared on the horizon and rescued them. Dudley and his crew admitted they'd killed and eaten the cabin boy, and when they returned to England they were arrested and tried for murder. They were found guilty and sentenced to death, but the sentence was later commuted to six months imprisonment. Afterwards, Tom Dudley emigrated to Australia, but his story doesn't have a happy ending – he became the first man in Australia to die from bubonic plague.

BUBONIC PLAGUE IN AUSTRALIA

Bubonic plague is transmitted to humans by fleas, and arrived in Australia – probably carried by rats in sailing ships – in January 1900. Spreading from the waterfront, the rats carried the plague throughout Sydney, and within eight months 303 cases were reported and 103 people were dead. Over 500 people died in total, and cases were still being reported ten years later.

There was no known cure for plague until streptomycin was discovered during the Second World War in 1943.

HUMan SacRiFice

Many peoples throughout history have believed that a god or gods controlled the world. To keep the gods happy, they developed rituals including offering the gods food and drink, sacrificing animals, and the most potent sacrifice of all – people.

In Greek mythology, the story of Theseus and the Minotaur tells how, every year, seven youths and seven maidens were sent to Crete to be sacrificed to a half-man, half-bull creature living inside a labyrinth. Theseus was a Greek prince who volunteered to be a sacrifice, but he managed to slay the Minotaur and find his way out of the labyrinth instead.

The Old Testament of the Christian Bible tells the story of Abraham preparing to sacrifice his son – until an angel spoke to him and suggested that a sheep would do instead.

In South and Central America, several civilisations developed religious human sacrifice on a grand scale.

central america

The Aztec people worshipped a sun god, Huitzilopochtli. They believed that without human sacrifices the sun might not rise, and the very existence of the universe could be under threat. This belief system became so central to the Aztec culture that they made war on neighbouring people to provide the human sacrifices the gods demanded.

Captives were sacrificed by ripping out their hearts while they were still alive, and the remains of the bodies were distributed to the Aztecs to be eaten. It is estimated that about 15,000 people a year were sacrificed, although on one special occasion, as many as 10,000 people were killed in a four-day festival dedicating the Great Temple in Tenochtitlan (in modern-day Mexico).

A thousand years before the Aztecs' gory ceremonies, the Mayas were also practising human sacrifice. The Mayas were the first people in Central America to develop writing, and their language included verbs such as 'decapitate', 'tear the heart out' and 'roll down the pyramid steps'. For more than 3000 years, the Mayan civilisation flourished. They developed a sophisticated calendar and erected large temple complexes and public buildings. They terraced hillsides and drained swamps for intensive farming, growing maize, beans, cotton and cacao. But just as the Mayan civilisation reached its peak, it disappeared. Within a century, cities were abandoned, monuments were toppled and burned, and the people melted into the jungle.

What happened to the Mayas has long been a mystery. Without lakes or rivers, the Mayas were dependent on annual rains and had developed a sophisticated system of waterways and reservoirs. Recent discoveries lead us to think that even this sophisticated water storage system was not enough to survive a long and terrible drought in the eighth century CE. With drought comes famine: people starve. They eat the seeds set aside to grow the next year's crops, they eat the animals, and then there's nothing left to eat. For a civilisation founded on religious ritual, it must have been a disaster. The people could only believe the gods were angry, and the priests with their prayers and sacrifices were absolutely no help. It still didn't rain. Did the starving people revolt and kill the priests and the ruling elite? Did they turn their backs on their great civilisation and walk away from the cities, searching for fertile land they could still farm?

WHAT YEAR IS IT?
(OR: TO BC OR NOT TO BCE)

The Christian dating system calculates years either side of the estimated year Christ was born. 'AD' is the abbreviation of the Latin for 'in the Year of our Lord', anno Domini. 'BC' is the abbreviation for 'before Christ'. Thus 1 AD is the year Christ was born, and 1 BC is the previous year. There is no year zero.

Recently people have become more sensitive to religious and cultural differences, and today you are just as likely to encounter dates written as 1 CE (the Common Era) or 1 BCE (Before the Common Era), as they are in this book.

The year 2000 CE still calculates 2000 years after the birth of Christ, but other cultures count their years differently. The year 2000 is the year 3760 in the Jewish calendar, 1421 for the Muslim calendar, 4636 for the Chinese calendar, 1921 for the Reformed Indian calendar, and 7508 for the Byzantine calendar (calculated from the estimated biblical creation of the world).

The first century of the Common Era is counted as the years from 1 CE to 100 CE, the second century from 101 to 200, and the twentieth century from 1901 to 2000. The first year of the twentieth-first century was 2001, and the last year will be 2100. As a quick calculation, centuries end with the year they are numbered multiplied by one hundred – so the sixth century ends with 600 CE, the sixteenth century with the year 1600 (and it includes the years 1501–1600), and 1867 falls in the nineteenth century, which ended with the year 1900. Dates Before the Common Era are calculated backwards: 100 BCE to 1 BCE for the first century, 200 BCE to 101 BCE for the second century, and so on.

Seasons are also calculated according to tradition and geography. Temperate climate zones recognise spring, summer, autumn and winter, while tropical climates have a wet season and a dry season. Australian Aborigines named their seasons after local climate, plants and animals.

The Kulin people living around Melbourne in southern Australia had seven seasons: Biderap Dry Season (when the tussock grass was dry in Jan-Feb), Iuk Eel (for harvesting eels), Waring Wombat (short days and long nights), Gulling Orchid (when these were in flower), Poorneet Tadpole (flax lilies in flower), Buath Guru Grass Flowering (kangaroo grass), and Kangaroo-Apple Season (long days and short nights).

CHOCOLATE

The Mayas left us an enduring legacy, apart from the mysteries of their great civilisation – chocolate! The Mayas were probably the first people to farm the cacao tree. They crushed the beans into a powder and mixed it into a ceremonial drink. Later, the Aztecs prized cacao beans so highly that they used them as currency. They also prepared a chocolate drink that they served after feasts in special cups.

The Spanish conquistador Hernan Cortez introduced the cacao bean to Europe. The Spanish thought the drink was too bitter, so they added sugar cane, vanilla and spices such as cinnamon and chilli. By the middle of the seventeenth century, chocolate was being drunk in fashionable coffee houses in Britain, and shortly afterwards it was mixed with hot milk and sugar – just like the hot chocolate we drink today.

Chocolate soon became a confectionary sweet as well as a drink, and in 1738 the first chocolate factory was built in London.

HOT CHOCOLATE MAYA STYLE

2 oz bitter chocolate • 1 cup hot water
3 tablespoons honey • 3 cups hot milk
4 sticks cinnamon

Carefully melt the chocolate with the hot water then add the honey.

Whisk the mixture as you add the hot milk and pour it into four cups. Serve with a cinnamon stick stirrer.

AUTHENTIC MAYAN HOT CHOCOLATE

COMBINE CHOCOLATE, HOT WATER, HONEY, MILK, AND CINNAMON. STIR. THEN RIP THE HEART OUT OF A HUMAN SACRIFICE & VOILA!

SOUTH AMERICA

The Inca Empire extended from modern-day Ecuador to southern Chile, and was at its peak from the twelfth century until the Spanish conquest several centuries later. The Incas also practised human sacrifice, including strangling, tearing out the heart and burying alive. They sacrificed children at their most sacred sites, including the tops of high mountains. Only the most beautiful and healthy children of noble birth were selected, and it was a great honour to be chosen, not only for the child but also for their family. The bodies of some of these children have been discovered in mountain tombs, their bodies and fine clothing perfectly preserved by the cold climate and high altitude.

DYING TO BE WITH YOU

Other civilisations practised human sacrifice as part of a burial ritual. The ancient Egyptians believed they would need companions and servants in the afterlife, so when the Pharaoh died, his slaves, soldiers and wives were often killed and buried with him to keep him company, and to continue to look after him in the next life. Early Chinese Emperors also took soldiers, wives and servants with them to their graves.

In India, Hindu widows were expected to commit suttee – committing suicide by throwing themselves on their dead husband's funeral pyre. Suttee was banned by the Moghul Emperors in the seventeenth century and made illegal under British rule in 1829, but at least forty cases of suttee have been suspected since India gained its independence from Britain in 1947.

SO THE STORY GOES . . .
WAS IT SUICIDE OR MURDER?

In 1996, in Rajasthan, thirty-two men were cleared of forcing a beautiful young widow to commit suttee nine years earlier. Roop Kanwar was nineteen years old when her husband died suddenly – they had been married only eight months and there were no children. The prospects for a young, childless widow in India were pretty grim: Kanwar would be expected to shave her head, wear simple white clothes, sleep on the floor and perform menial tasks for the rest of her life.

On the morning of her husband's funeral, Kanwar

appeared dressed in her beautiful wedding sari and jewellery. A procession of more than 500 villagers followed her to the cremation ground, where she climbed the funeral pyre and laid her head on her husband's body. The fire was lit, and the villagers reported that she died with a beautiful smile on her face. They rejoiced in the young widow's sacrifice, believing she had brought good luck to her family and village for the next seven generations. Others disagreed with the reported events, claiming Kanwar was dragged screaming through the village by a mob of fanatical villagers, and was drugged with opium before being forced to join her husband's body on the funeral pyre. The police investigated and charged thirty-seven villagers with murder. The trial took almost a decade to complete, by which time five defendants had already died.

A few weeks after Kanwar's death, over 750,000 people had turned up to worship at the site of her pyre, but by the time the villagers were cleared of murder, all that was left was a small shrine covered with cobwebs and dust.

A BRieF HiSTORY OF SLaVeRY

One man's unacceptable behaviour is another man's civilisation, and for much of history, slavery has been accepted as a normal part of society. Indeed, many people have vigorously defended the institution of slavery as being absolutely essential.

Slavery probably first began in prehistoric times, when a captive was brought home from a raid. The captive did what she was told if she wanted to stay alive, and sooner or later she was probably accepted into the tribe. But slavery as an institution didn't really get going until people became more organised. Big armies can capture a lot of people, and when you have a lot of captives, it's easier to set them apart and make them live by different rules. Ancient Egyptians used captives as slaves, though very few Egyptians themselves were enslaved, and normally only as a punishment. Ancient China seems to have developed much the same system: captives and criminals were enslaved, but ordinary people were not. Slaves worked for nothing and belonged to their master; ordinary people had to be paid for their labour (even if it wasn't very much) and got to go home afterwards.

BUILDING ON THE BACK OF SLAVES

Greece and Rome both practised slavery. Not only could captives and criminals be enslaved, but people could choose to sell themselves into slavery because of their debts, or just because they were poor and had no other way to support themselves.

LOOK - I CAN'T REPAY MY HOME LOAN — WHAT IF I BECOME YOUR SLAVE?

MANAGER

In ancient Athens in the seventh century BCE, a few rich and powerful families controlled the city, buying up all the land from the small farmers, so the rich became richer and the poor became poorer. Finally, so many Athenians sold themselves into debt slavery that there was a crisis. Civil war loomed. The Athenians appointed a poet to see if he could sort out the mess, and Solon became the lawgiver of Athens: he forgave all outstanding debt and forbade further debt slavery. He returned the land to the farmers and made them free citizens, and then he made them eligible to hold a government position. Athens went on to develop the concept of democracy and the high culture of ancient Greece. (And philosophy and mathematics and architecture and sculpture and history and literature and a questioning mind and an appreciation for beauty.)

But all was not rosy in ancient Greece. The philosopher Aristotle wrote:

'Humanity is divided into two: the masters and the slaves; or, if one prefers it, the Greeks and the Barbarians, those who have the right to command and those who were born to obey.'

Slaves worked as domestic servants, in mines and on farms, as well as on the construction of roads and buildings, creating artworks and teaching. A few people swam against the tide; another Greek philosopher observed that:

'The man who relied on captive labour was the true slave.'

But objectors were in the minority. Slaves did just about everything, and when the Roman Empire took over from the Greeks, Rome became dependent on the slave. Half a million captives were required every year to keep Rome running during its heyday – for more than two and a half centuries. The few Roman critics seemed to be more concerned with cruelty to slaves than the institution of slavery itself.

FROM SLAVE TO SERF

The early Christian Church didn't exactly ban slavery, though it encouraged people to treat slaves well, and promised slaves they could look forward to freedom in the next world. And the Church encouraged people to free slaves, particularly those who converted to Christianity.

Over the next few centuries, the institution of slavery gradually died out in much of Europe. Instead, the feudal system introduced the social position of 'serf'. Unlike slaves, serfs could not be bought or sold, but they were 'bonded' to the land and their master. Serfs couldn't leave without their master's permission, but they were responsible for their own upkeep and welfare. They worked the master's land a few days a week without getting paid, then spent the rest of the week trying to feed and clothe themselves and their families. This system may well have suited the master better than slavery: he wasn't responsible for the daily welfare of his serfs, he still got their labour free, and they couldn't just get up and leave if they didn't like it. It wasn't until the Black Death ravaged Europe that this system changed.

Black Death Kills Serfs

Between one third and one half of the population of Europe died of bubonic plague during the Black Plague in the fourteenth and fifteenth centuries. Whole villages died out and were abandoned. The countryside was depopulated and there were not enough people left to work the land. Serfs began to shift to find work. They discovered that one landowner would pay them more than another, so they shifted again. The landowners didn't like all this shifting around, so they passed new laws to try to prevent serfs from leaving their land; but it was too late – the serfs had already left.

Slavery hadn't disappeared altogether, but by now most of Europe and Asia was acquainted with the practice of 'acquiring' slaves, and they were well prepared to defend themselves (or hide at the first sight of the slavers). The 'black slave' from Africa became more popular. The Arabs had conquered North Africa and opened up slave trade routes across the Sahara to Morocco, and from there around the Mediterranean. In 1444, a new African cargo was landed in Portugal – 235 slaves.

Slavery was a new experience for most tribal Africans, and many slaves were kidnapped or captured by trickery.

The high prices offered for captured slaves only encouraged other Africans to help supply the trade. Local tribes
often assisted the slavers, and indeed, some African tribes
had practised slavery themselves
before the traders from
the north arrived.

Within two hundred years, slavery in Europe came to
an end. The local birthrate had risen and they didn't need
the labour. But there was somewhere that did.

THere's Money to Be Made in slaves

The 'discovery' of the New World brought slavery back to
the Europeans. Landowners needed labour to work their
vast new properties, and the slave trade shifted from
Europe, transporting black slaves directly from Africa to
the Americas and beyond.

These were dreadful voyages. The slaves were branded
with hot irons and shackled together, the left wrist and
ankle of one slave bound to the right wrist and ankle of
the slave next to him. The ships were overcrowded and
the slaves were jammed in like sardines, with only just

enough room to lie down and not enough room to stand up. Without proper sanitation and decent food, the death toll was terrible. They died from scurvy, smallpox, dysentery and a multitude of other nasty diseases. Some slaves committed suicide by jumping overboard; others refused to eat, at which point the 'valuable cargo' would be force-fed. Sick or injured slaves were thrown overboard to drown.

By the middle of the eighteenth century, many Europeans were making a fortune out of the slave trade – not only the traders themselves, but the shipyards and shipbuilders busy with orders for new ships. The European colonial settlers in Jamaica and North America were growing wealthy using slaves to work their new crops of tobacco, cotton and coffee. And Europe began to use these raw materials to fire up their new industries. Traders from North America began to enter the slave market directly, instead of dealing with Arab slavers. All in all it was a cosy little arrangement and everyone was getting rich – except the slaves.

Freeing the Slaves?

By the late eighteenth century, people had begun to talk about the morality of slavery. It was the beginning of the Age of Enlightenment, and before the century was out, slavery had been denounced across most of Europe. Denmark banned slave trading in 1802 and Britain in 1807; Spain banned slave trading in 1820, except for its colony in Cuba where slavery wasn't banned until 1886. President Lincoln freed slaves during the middle of the American Civil War in 1863.

Yet slavery has still not disappeared completely – Saudi Arabia only banned slavery in 1962 – and every year there are still reports of illegal slave trading.

In February 1998, an American fifth-grade teacher, Barbara Vogel, read her class an article about the enslavement of blacks in the south of Sudan. John Eibner from Christian Solidarity International had testified before the United Nations Human Rights Commission about:

'the astonishing revival at the close of the twentieth century of chattel slavery in Sudan.'

He described the conditions:

'severe beatings, acute hunger, forced conversion (to Islam), rape and ritual female genital mutilation. These horrors . . . are the grim reality for the tens of thousands of children and young mothers who are now in bondage.'

Barbara Vogel's class were horrified, and when they heard that Christian Solidarity International had bought back slaves from their captors and returned them to their homes, they started to save their pocket money. At the time, slaves in Sudan were going at a price of about US$100 per head. The Denver school children continued to collect money, eventually raising about US$9000 – enough to release 150 to 160 slaves. But there were unexpected side effects. The sudden demand pushed up the price of slaves, and the traders used the profits to buy more slaves. Some of the money just disappeared and was never used to help the slaves. The well-meaning school children were actually helping to keep the slave trade alive. A spokeswoman from UNICEF explained their position:

'The practice of paying for the retrieval of enslaved children and women does not address the underlying causes of slavery in Sudan: the ongoing civil war and its by-products of criminality. Until these root problems are addressed, there can be no lasting solution.'

Racism

Although slaves were freed during the American Civil War, it was not the end of difficult times for African-Americans. Many Americans were still suspicious of 'coloured' people. Even President Lincoln didn't believe that whites and blacks could live together in peace, and was in favour of relocating the black population. Some communities segregated blacks from whites, expecting black people to use separate doorways, sit at the back of the bus, or even to be totally excluded from 'white' schools, shops and neighbourhoods. It was a form of apartheid – a policy of segregating people by the colour of their skin.

In 1954 the American Supreme Court ruled that all legal segregation was unconstitutional. Separating children in schools because of their skin colour left coloured children feeling inferior, and was a violation of the 'equal protection' amendment in the constitution.

Not everyone in America agreed. Groups that supported racial hatred (such as the Ku Klux Klan) began a campaign of violence and intimidation. In many southern states there were bombings, beatings and even murder. It came to a head three years later in Little Rock, Arkansas, when the American president sent in troops for the first time to enforce the law and coloured children's right to attend 'white' schools.

On 1 December 1955, Mrs Rosa Parks was travelling home on a bus after a hard day at work. She lived in the town of Montgomery in Alabama in the south of America. As the bus gradually filled up with passengers, a white man boarded the bus and demanded that Mrs Parks should give him her seat and stand up in the back of the bus. Mrs Parks was black. Her feet hurt and she was tired, so she refused. The white man complained to the bus driver, and he also told Mrs Parks to shift. She refused again. The driver called a policeman and Mrs Parks was arrested and dragged off the bus. Many Americans were outraged. They believed Mrs Parks was a hardworking woman who was completely innocent and had been mistreated and humiliated by the incident. She certainly didn't deserve to be arrested. Protest meetings were held, and a lot of protesters agreed to boycott the buses in Montgomery. A young Baptist minister was chosen to lead the first bus boycott. His name was Martin Luther King, and he believed in a philosophy of non-violent protest. In his famous speech he declared:

'I have a dream that one day on the red hills of Georgia the sons of former slaves and the sons of former slave-

owners will be able to sit down together at the table of
brotherhood ... I have a dream that my four little
children will one day live in a nation where they will
not be judged by the colour of their skin, but by the
content of their character.'

The bus boycott dragged on for months – black people
refused to travel on buses, and soon the bus company in
Montgomery was losing money. Mass protests spread
throughout America, and eventually the bus company
was forced to change its policy of segregated seating:
black people could sit anywhere they liked. In 1964 the
USA passed the Civil Rights Act enshrining the rights of
individual citizens – there was no difference between
black and white citizens. Dr King was awarded the Nobel
Peace Prize in the same year. But not everyone agreed
with the changes that were taking place, and in 1968
Martin Luther King was assassinated. His death did not
stop the civil rights movement, but even today racial
hatred is alive in the USA. In 1998 in Jasper, Texas, three
white men chained a black man, James Byrd Jr, to the
back of their pick-up truck and dragged him to his death,
just because he was black.

Save tHe CHILDRen

Throughout history, there have always been children who
worked for a living. As long as children didn't work under
unhealthy conditions and had free time to play and
receive some sort of education, it was not necessarily a
bad thing. There were no schools for poor children, and
their families needed their help with the family farm or
business, or they needed their wages just to survive.

But during the eighteenth century a new social problem arose – the exploitation of child labour for financial gain. With the beginning of industrialisation, factory owners needed more workers. Children were ideal for much factory work. They were small and agile, and they were cheap to employ. They were unlikely to form trade unions or go on strike. They were easy to control.

Children were sent down coalmines to work long hours in dark tunnels under extremely unhealthy conditions.

WHY DON'T YOU GO DOWN THAT COAL MINE? I THINK THERE ARE LOLLIES AT THE BOTTOM!

They were forced to climb up chimneys to sweep them out and clean them. They worked among noisy, dirty, dangerous machinery. Many children under the age of ten worked for more than twelve hours a day, and there were heavy fines if they were late for work. They ate their lunch standing up and went straight back to work. They were hit with a strap to make them work faster, beaten if they were disobedient, and doused with water if they fell asleep. The girls had their hair cut off if they spoke to boys. They were chained up if they threatened to run away, and they were often killed or maimed in factory accidents.

Many children had no parents or their parents were

unable to support them, and a system of apprenticeships for 'pauper children' sprang up in England under the 'Poor Laws'. Factory owners could 'purchase' the labour of children, and apprentice contracts bound the children to the factory until they were twenty-one years old. Apprentice factory workers lived together in cramped housing, fed on a diet of porridge, bread and potatoes, and were locked up when they weren't working. Children became sick and died. It was a terrible life.

In the nineteenth century, social reformers began to speak out against child labour. Gradually new laws were passed for the protection of children working in factories, until finally, in 1878, the Factory Acts were passed by parliament. These Acts raised the age at which children could start work, shortened their working hours, and generally improved safety and conditions.

In 1973, an International Labour Organisation (ILO) Convention set the minimum age for work as fifteen years except in poor countries without adequate schools, where children twelve years old could undertake light work, and fourteen heavier work. Recently the ILO estimated that there are between 100 and 200 million children working around the world. It is estimated that more than ninety-five per cent of these children are employed in developing countries. Most children are forced to work because they are economically disadvantaged – their families or their countries are poor. Many developing countries have a large population of young people, and their labour is needed to make up the work force. Children are still cheap to employ. Their families often desperately need the money from their wages, and factory owners still enjoy the profits to be had from cheap and obedient workers.

Today, most child labourers work either in small-scale

agriculture, manufacturing, prostitution, or service industries. They work as servants, field hands, street vendors, and factory and mining workers. Their labour is often a significant part of their country's economy. Governments are reluctant to enforce child labour laws because they fear manufacturers will shift their factories to another country if the workers cost too much, which would further disadvantage their country. Poor countries need an educated work force, but while children work long hard days, they are unable to attend school. Just like the slave trade, child labour is a difficult and vexing problem.

SO THE STORY GOES . . .
PLEASE, SIR, I WANT SOME MORE

The English author Charles Dickens began work in a factory when he was twelve. His father had been thrown in jail for unpaid debts, and Charles had to support the family until his father was released. Dickens published his first story in 1833. He often wrote about the lives of poor children at the time, and exposed the horrible conditions they lived under. One of his most famous books is *Oliver Twist*, the story of a young pauper boy who escapes a cruel workhouse where he has been locked up for daring to ask for more food, only to become caught up in a life of crime. Fortunately for Oliver, the book has a happy ending – the reality for many children at the time was not so rosy.

Dickens became a best-selling author. His readers not only enjoyed his great characters and dramatic stories, but also were horrified by the terrible reality of poor people's lives. Dickens's writing would help set the scene for popular social reform.

WOMEN ARE PEOPLE TOO

Throughout history, women have generally had fewer rights and opportunities than men, and indeed many cultures still view women and children as chattels – pieces of property. Even today, it has been estimated that women do about 65 per cent of the world's work, while they own only 10 per cent of the wealth and less than 1 per cent of the land. How did this inequality come to be?

Some people claim that men are physically stronger than women are, and should therefore be in control. Others suggest that women have the babies and are naturally more vulnerable. However, prehistoric evidence does not support this theory. Before animals and crops were domesticated, women seem to have held much the same status as men – both sexes were responsible for the gathering of food, women are depicted in art and sculpture, and their graves are as elaborately decorated as those of men.

But when the nomadic hunter-gatherers settled down, things began to change. Where once women were responsible for gathering wild grains and hunting small animals, men began to dominate food production, ploughing the fields and herding the animals. Women stayed home to look after the children and attend to the new domestic chores of cooking, cleaning and the production of textiles. This new lifestyle produced a surplus of food and goods, which could be bought and sold, and the concept of ownership evolved. Not only could goods be exchanged or purchased, but women and children could also be traded. Men could get rich.

Women's role in societies also changed over time. Even though ancient Egypt was a male-dominated society, ordinary women had rights, they could own land and enter into contracts and retain their property if they divorced their husbands. In the early history of the Mesopotamian Empire, women's rights were not equal to men's, but they could own land and engage in business. But eventually an enormous gap opened up between the rights of high and low status women in the Middle East. During the Assyrian Empire (2500–612 BCE, centred in modern-day Iraq) women's rights and freedoms quickly eroded. The first laws were introduced that required high-status women to wear veils in public, and the practice was soon adopted by the lower classes.

Hinduism evolved in India after 500 BCE, and it required women to be obedient to men. Women had to walk behind their husbands, they could not own property, and widows were forbidden to remarry. Women in ancient Athens, wrote one Greek writer:

'were always minors, subject to some male – to their father, to their brother, or to some male kin.'

A woman in ancient Rome was considered the property of the male head of the household – her father, brother, husband or even her son. Women could not hold public office, or make a will or a contract.

The early Christian Church contributed to the low status of women, teaching that it was Eve, a woman, who was responsible for man's downfall and his expulsion from the Garden of Eden. St Jerome wrote in the fourth century:

'Woman is the gate of the devil; the path of wickedness, the sting of the serpent, in a word a perilous object.'

Women were considered to be evil temptresses, sent by the devil to lure men away from God. Things weren't much better in the thirteenth century when another Christian writer, Thomas Aquinas, declared:

'Woman was created to be man's helpmate.'

WE'RE OUT OF ARMCHAIRS —BE A GOOD WIFE & LET MR. RICHARDS SIT ON YOU, WON'T YOU DARLING.

In Europe, until the eighteenth century, women had almost no legal rights. Their lives were controlled by their father, or, if they married, by their husband. Women were not allowed to go to university, they were not allowed to enter a profession, and any property or money they did have could be legally controlled by their husbands. Even the early evolutionists tried to suggest that women were biologically and intellectually inferior to men. It was no wonder that women made little headway with their struggle for equality.

With the abolition of slavery at the start of the nineteenth century, women began to agitate for their rights. A British philosopher, John Stuart Mill, entered parliament and became a champion for women's rights. In 1869, he published a book called *On the Subjection of Women* which was influential in changing the way people thought about the position of women in society. But it was not until 1882 that the Married Women's Property Act was passed in the British parliament, allowing a married woman to retain ownership of any property that was given to her by her parents.

It was only the start. Women wanted more; they

wanted the right to go to school, to have professional jobs, and they wanted the right to vote. The suffragette movement began in England as women (and a few men) began to agitate for female suffrage – the right for women to vote. During the last years of the nineteenth century and the beginning of the twentieth century, many attempts were made to introduce new laws in the British parliament that would allow women to vote, but they were all defeated. A group of women decided to use more drastic tactics, and in 1905 Emmeline Pankhurst launched a militant campaign for female suffrage. The suffragettes made noisy protests and chained themselves to the railings outside parliament. One woman was killed when she rushed in front of a horse race to protest. Women were arrested and sent to prison, and they went on hunger strikes in protest. The prison authorities had them force-fed: tied up while a rubber tube was forced down their throats and food poured down the tube. Sometimes the tube went into the women's lungs instead of their stomachs. Still women did not get the vote.

But the First World War interrupted the suffragette movement. The resulting labour shortage, when so many men were sent to fight and die, meant that women had to work. Britain needed strong, educated women to fill all the vacant jobs. They needed women to work on the farms, to drive tractors and trucks and buses. They needed skilled women to work in the factories producing armaments for the war. They needed doctors and nurses, teachers and scientists. At the end of the war in 1918, women achieved limited suffrage (some women could vote), and a decade later all women over twenty-one were given the vote in Britain.

But the struggle is not over in other countries. Just

like the abolition of slavery and child labour laws, the emancipation of women is a difficult and vexing question. Many societies rely on the unpaid labour of women. Families, farming communities and small family businesses often rely on the work that women perform for nothing. Other cultures require women to live separate lives. The universal emancipation of women would upset many economic and cultural traditions.

The right to vote is just the beginning. Women all over the world are still working for equality – to enjoy the same rights and freedoms as men.

LET'S VOTE

New Zealand was the first country to give women the vote in 1893, followed by Australia in 1902, Finland in 1906, Norway in 1913, Denmark and Iceland in 1915, Canada in 1917, and many other countries soon after, including the USA in 1920, Spain in 1931, Brazil in 1934, the Philippines in 1937, and Italy and Japan in 1945. In Africa, women were often enfranchised (given the right to vote) at the same time as men – Liberia in

1947, and Uganda in 1958. Women still cannot vote in some Middle Eastern countries such as Saudi Arabia and Kuwait. Aboriginal peoples of Australia were not enfranchised until 1967.

Law and Order

The right of citizens to participate in government – to hold political offices and vote – first began back in ancient Greece. (It's where the word democracy comes from.) But in ancient Greece, not everyone was considered to be a citizen. Slaves couldn't vote. Women couldn't vote. In fact, only men who owned land and were native citizens of the city could vote and participate in government.

Rome was a republic at first, and, like ancient Greece, only male citizens of certain families could sit in the Senate and vote. But Rome became an empire, ruled by emperors with the power of life and death over the citizens, and democracy fell into decline. It was the time of princes and kings.

Ancient kings ruled by divine right (they were direct representatives of gods) or by force (their armies were bigger and meaner), which pretty much meant there was almost no check on their powers. Roman emperors sentenced people to death on a whim, and apart from a direct appeal to the emperor there was almost nothing you could do about it. The king's (emperor's) word was law. Of course, people did regularly seek other solutions – they raised armies, or assassinated the king – but they almost always just put another king on the throne. If you were lucky, he was a good king; if he wasn't, you had to start the whole process over again.

LiMiTiNG THE KiNG'S POWER

Nearly eight hundred years ago, King John of England was forced to sign a document that limited his royal powers. When King John signed the Magna Carta, he introduced the first laws protecting ordinary people from royal excesses and abuse. Over the years, the Magna Carta has become a symbol of human rights, freedom, liberty and equality. It paved the way for legal systems and the rule of law and eventually written constitutions – documents outlining how a country is to be governed and how the government will work.

Of course, ordinary people aren't even mentioned in the Magna Carta. It was the rich and influential nobles who wanted to limit the king's power. They wanted freedom for the Church to elect bishops without interference from the king. They wanted to limit the amount of land the king could claim for himself. They wanted laws about money and debts, and other laws about merchants and the City of London. No mention of ordinary people there. But it was a beginning.

Four copies of the original Magna Carta still exist. One was signed and sealed by King John and is safely stored in Lincoln Cathedral in England. Two others are lodged at the British Museum, and one is on display at Salisbury Cathedral.

SeParaTioN oF PoWeR

Polybius was an ancient Greek historian who thought a lot about how governments worked and why they might become corrupt and fail. He believed that hereditary succession – the handing down of power and privilege from one generation to the next – was the root of the problem. His theory goes something like this.

In a monarchy, any new king who comes to the throne by his own endeavours has already proved he is at least brave and intelligent enough to seize power. He is motivated to be a successful king and generally governs well. But over the years, as his children and his children's children inherit the throne, they are no longer selected because they are brave and intelligent people, but by an accident of birth. Even worse, because they've been raised to a life of privilege and luxury, they are likely to be interested only in themselves. They become greedy and arrogant. The king becomes a tyrant and will eventually be overthrown by those people closest to him – the aristocracy who have observed the king's greed and arrogance at close quarters.

At first the aristocracy governs well – remember, they were the people who overthrew the king to put a stop to his greedy excesses – but, over the years, their children and their children's children are raised to a life of privilege and inherited power. Now a small group of people rule – an oligarchy. They haven't spoken to an ordinary person in years. They are only interested in governing for themselves, and they become greedy and arrogant.

Finally the people take matters into their own hands, overthrow their rulers and set up a democracy. At first the people govern well. But over the years they forget what it was like to live under any other form of government. They become complacent about the privileges and responsibilities of democracy. Once ordinary people cease to be involved and stop guarding their democratic rights, individuals eventually rise to seize power and make themselves tyrants and kings. And the whole cycle begins again.

Polybius believed that republican Rome almost got it right when it established a mixed constitution that included, but also limited, the powers of each group: the monarchy (a regularly elected ruler), the aristocrats (the Senate) and democracy (assemblies that gave ordinary people some say). He believed that sharing power between three separate groups prevented the corrupting influence of absolute power.

CONSTITUTION OF THE UNITED STATES OF AMERICA

The USA has the oldest written constitution in the world. America was originally a British colony, but in 1775 the American people finally got sick of the high taxes imposed by the British, and they revolted. For seven years they fought and finally won a war for their independence, and in 1787 the Constitution of the United States of America was signed. It limits the power of government by the separation of powers, in this case into the executive, the legislature and the judiciary. Very simply, the President is the executive and makes decisions about running the country, but he must do this in accordance with the laws made by the elected representatives of the legislature or Congress (which he does not control). In turn, the Congress must have their laws tested by the independent judiciary (judges) to make sure they are in accordance with the constitution. Each group checks and limits the powers of the other. At its best, that's the way it's supposed to work.

CHina sets Exams

Ancient China was ruled by kings (or emperors) who generally got the job by military might when they overthrew the existing royal family. These new kings were often from humble origins and had little education, but it didn't take them long to realise that conquering a kingdom was only the first problem – next they had to govern. They needed an army of educated civil servants to collect taxes and administer the government.

The great Chinese philosopher Confucius believed that social harmony could only be achieved if people were educated. He also believed that all people possessed the same potential, and so education was made available to students of all the social classes. The first state system of education in China was founded before the first century BCE, and within a hundred years the first Imperial Examinations were taking place. They would continue for the next two thousand years.

STUDY or Die

The Imperial Examinations were pretty tough. The exams could last anywhere from twenty-four to seventy-two hours. Scholars would travel long distances to take an exam, and sometimes a whole village sponsored a candidate. The candidate would take the exam in a very small room that contained only a bench for sleeping and a desk with a lamp (for writing all night) and writing materials. Most candidates failed, and at times the pass rate was about two per cent. Some candidates continued to re-sit the exams until they were old men, while others committed suicide because of the disgrace their failure brought to their family.

Scholars studied the Confucian classics and sat exams in music, archery and horsemanship, arithmetic, writing and general knowledge, as well as the ceremonies of private and public life. Later they sat exams in military strategies, civil law, revenue and taxation, agriculture and geography. They were expected to write poetry and analyse political problems. Candidates were required to memorise vast amounts of information, but for those candidates who passed, not only would they get a good job, their families and villages would also benefit financially from the prestige of a successful candidate.

'To enrich your family, there is no need to buy good land: books hold a thousand measures of grain. For an easy life, there is no need to build a mansion: in books are found houses of gold.'
                                        (Old Chinese saying)

Unfortunately, all that rote learning and memorising didn't encourage students to question and dispute what they were learning. It was not until the Renaissance – the revival of artistic, literary and scientific achievements that flowered during the fifteenth and sixteenth centuries – that the first medieval universities were opened in Europe and students were encouraged to debate and ask questions. At its height, the Renaissance gave birth to such geniuses as Michelangelo, Leonardo da Vinci, William Shakespeare, Copernicus and Galileo, and it paved the way for the development of the modern world.

IMPRESS YOUR FRIENDS

People have been changing and attempting to change governments by various means for so long that there are special words to describe them. Amaze and impress your friends with a few of them.

Sedition – inciting hostility against a government, likely to cause rebellion or insurrection, but not amounting to treason.

Rebellion – an organised attempt to overthrow a government by force of arms.

Revolt – opposing a government, especially by armed rebellion.

Insurrection – organised opposition to authority.

Treason – an organised attempt to overthrow a government by illegal means, or working with enemies of the state.

Insurgent – a rebel opposed to a lawful government.

Mutiny – open revolt against lawful authority, especially with regard to the navy and army.

Coup d'état (or coup) – based on the idea of cutting off the head. A forcible and often violent overthrow of the government by a small group of people from within the country.

Unlike a revolution, it is not a popular uprising. Coups can be successful or unsuccessful.

Putsch – German word for coup d'état.

Tyrannicide – the act of killing a tyrant (an oppressive and cruel ruler).

Regicide – the crime of killing a monarch.

Monarch – a person ruling by hereditary means for his/her lifetime over a kingdom of people.

Quisling – a person who collaborates with an occupying enemy power. Named after a Norwegian politician (Vidkun Quisling) who aided the Nazi takeover of Norway during World War II. He was arrested and shot in 1945.

Tergiversator – someone who changes sides, especially if it involves desertion.

Insubordination – not submitting to authority.

Purge – to remove undesirable elements (people suspected of opposing the people in power) from a political party, armed forces or government.

Lese-majesty – an offence against the dignity of the sovereign.

Revolting

The first popular revolution of modern times was the American revolution against British rule (the War of Independence). 'Popular' here means 'of the people' – everyone got involved – rather than the more modern meaning that everyone just sat around thinking it was a good idea. The French Revolution followed just over a decade later when the French people overthrew King Louis XVI. The Russian Revolution didn't get under way until 1917. The Chinese Revolution began with a series of popular uprisings in 1911, which expanded to open civil war between 1946 and 1949, and finally established communist rule under Mao Tse-Tung.

Throw a Party

Other countries achieved their independence with a party rather than a war.

On 1 January 1901, the Commonwealth of Australia was created with the signing of a document, and everyone celebrated with a big party. Australia now had its own constitution and its own parliament. The city streets were decorated with banners and flags for parades. Brass bands played for the crowds watching the procession of school children, soldiers on horseback, churchmen, politicians and fire brigades. The new governor-general read out the proclamation and signed the papers in front of a crowd of 70,000 people in Centennial Park in Sydney. There were official banquets and singing and fireworks and dancing and a lot of drinking.

A few months later, the parties continued in Melbourne when the first parliament was opened. There were more banquets and parades and parties as people celebrated in the streets, which had been decorated with electric lights especially for the occasion.

BURN DOWN a PUB

The only armed rebellion in Australia had its beginning on the goldfields, when the miners burned down a pub – the Eureka Hotel.

People from all over the world flocked to make their fortunes in Australia during the gold rush. Some of the richest goldfields were around Ballarat, Victoria. The government imposed an expensive licence fee on the diggers, and the troopers enforced it brutally, raiding the miners' camps and arresting anyone without a licence.

The diggers were very unhappy, and on 29 November 1854, nearly 12,000 protestors gathered to listen to speakers call for an end to the unfair licence system and government corruption. They raised a flag and demanded representation in the Victorian parliament, swearing to fight for the 'Victorian Republic'. They built a stockade and passed out guns.

This was treason. The government moved swiftly and sent in the troopers who stormed the stockade at dawn on Sunday 3 December. It was all over after a short fifteen-minute battle and the rebels were defeated. Fifteen people were killed and another thirteen wounded. When the leaders of the rebellion were tried for treason, the juries refused to convict them and they were all acquitted. The Victorian Government abolished the gold licence system and gave the miners the vote and parliamentary representation.

SO THE STORY GOES . . .
AN AUSTRALIAN LEGEND

Born in the same year as the Eureka Stockade, Australia's most famous bushranger made his own protest about the corruption and unfairness of the system. Ned Kelly was the third of eight children in a poor Irish family. When Ned was twelve years old, his father died and he had to support the family. Government policy of the time forced many poor families off their land, and, like many others, Ned resorted to stealing horses and cattle and petty crime just to survive. He received three years jail for horse stealing, and shortly after he was released, there was more trouble. Ned became convinced the police were persecuting his family.

After the family home was raided and his mother was arrested and sent to jail, Ned, along with members of his family and friends, fled to the bush. The police went in after them, and, after a shoot-out, three policemen lay dead. Now Ned Kelly and his gang were outlaws and the most hunted men in all Australia. A huge reward was put on Ned's head. The Kelly gang robbed banks before melting into the bush. They held up the bank at Jerilderie, captured two policemen, and herded the sixty people living in the town into the local hotel. Ned dictated a long letter in the Jerilderie pub in which he explained and justified his crimes, describing the police's behaviour as:

'brutal and cowardly conduct of a parcel of big ugly fat-necked wombat headed big bellied magpie legged narrow hipped splaw-footed sons of Irish Bailiffs or english landlords which is better known as Officers of Justice or Victorian Police who some calls honest gentlemen...'

Finally, Ned called on the rich to give money to widows, orphans and the poor, declaring:

'I am a widows son
outlawed
and my orders
must be obeyed.'

GIVE ME ALL
YOUR MONEY
—— AND A
CAN-OPENER
IF YOU HAVE
ONE...

The next time the Kelly gang struck the small township of Glenrowan, the local schoolteacher escaped and warned the police, who surrounded the town. There was a shoot-out, and even though Ned was protected by homemade armour, the police shot him in the legs and captured the outlaw. Ned Kelly was tried and sentenced to death. On 11 November 1880, he was hanged in the Old Melbourne Gaol.

Executions

Torture and capital punishment have a long historical tradition. The Babylonians used the death penalty for such crimes as the fraudulent sale of beer. The Egyptians imposed the death penalty for disclosing the location of sacred places.

The ancient Romans believed that while a citizen might tell the truth when questioned, slaves were of such low moral character that they would only tell the truth under torture. By law, slaves had to be tortured when questioned. Roman execution methods for capital crimes included being thrown from a cliff and crucifixion. Rome was a patriarchal society, and for the crime of patricide (murdering your father) the death sentence was severe. The criminal was sewn into a sack with a rooster, a dog, and a snake, and thrown into the sea to drown.

The Christian Church picked up the torture theme. They believed that witches and heretics (people who didn't agree with the current church teachings) could only be saved by confession, and the best way to wring a confession out of anyone was torture. For such suspicious crimes as your neighbour's milk turning sour (!), suspected witches were left alone in a small, dark, damp cell for days, weeks, months or even longer. But sooner or later they were dragged to the torture chamber, stripped and bound, and subjected to the most unimaginable horrors.

First the torturer would show the victim the instruments of his profession: the red-hot pincers, the rack, the wheel, the thumbscrews, the garrotting chair, the bed of nails (to name just a few). If this didn't induce the witch to confess, she would be tortured until she did. She would then be tortured again until she confessed the names of other witches. (Much the same theory applied to heretics.) The end result was that the inquisitor had a new list of names to begin torturing all over again.

It wasn't the end of agony for the convicted witch or heretic. Methods of execution were as horrible as the torture – those condemned to die could be crucified, flayed alive, boiled alive, crushed, burnt at the stake, disembowelled, torn apart, locked in a cage and left to starve, bludgeoned and mutilated, hoisted on a wheel and left to die while the crows picked out their eyes. All of these were conducted as a public spectacle.

After the Age of Enlightenment, more 'humane' methods of execution were introduced: the guillotine, the hangman's noose and the firing squad. Eventually these were no longer public, although official witnesses would still watch the execution. Many states in the USA still apply the death penalty, and modern methods of execution include the gas chamber, the electric chair and lethal injection. And although many other countries have abolished the death penalty, torture and capital punishment still take place all over the world today.

SO THE STORY GOES . . .
THE MAN WHO ESCAPED THE NOOSE

In 1884, John Lee had been found guilty of the murder of a woman in Devonshire, England. He was sentenced to death and taken to Exeter prison. The gallows were set up and the public executioner checked the rope and the trapdoor beneath; he'd already made his calculations for a quick, clean hanging. Everything was ready and the condemned man was blindfolded and led out onto the gallows. The noose was placed around John Lee's neck, the executioner stepped back and pulled the lever to open the trapdoor. Nothing happened. The prisoner was taken off the scaffold while the executioner jumped up and down on the trapdoor until he was satisfied it was working. By now John Lee was shaking with terror, but once again they returned him to the gallows and placed the noose around his neck. The mechanism failed. They tried again for a third time, and still the trapdoor failed. By now everyone was so upset that they returned the prisoner to his cell. The matter was referred to the courts, and it was decided that John Lee had already suffered enough, and his sentence was commuted to life imprisonment. Eventually John Lee was released from prison, and he emigrated to the USA.

WHERE TO NEXT?

Cannibalism, human sacrifice, slavery, torture – what was acceptable thousands of years ago, or even a decade ago, is often not acceptable today. And no doubt there are behaviours we take for granted in today's society that our descendants in the future will think of as barbaric. Hard to believe? What about eating meat? Logging trees? Locking up drug addicts and refugees? Most of us accept these activities as a normal part of society, but other people passionately believe they are wrong. Who knows which way the wheel of history will turn?

ACCIDENTAL HEROES

(AND VILLAINS)

DISASTER ON THE POTOMAC

The thirteenth of January 1982 brought Washington DC one of its worst winter storms in decades. It was so cold even the Potomac River cutting through the city had frozen over. Washington National Airport was closed briefly in the morning, but it reopened at lunchtime. Schools and businesses were closing early, and the roads and bridges were packed with traffic as people tried to get home before another blizzard rolled in. Passengers at the airport climbed aboard Air Florida's non-stop flight to sunny Florida, glad to be leaving behind the freezing grey Washington weather. They stowed their carry-on bags, took out their magazines and made themselves comfortable. In the cockpit, the pilots ran through the pre-flight checklist, while the cabin crew settled the passengers and ran through the emergency disaster routine. There were seventy-nine people on board.

The blue-and-green airliner waited on the snow-covered runway for clearance to take off – Air Florida Flight 90 was already over an hour and a half behind schedule. The freezing weather was causing problems, and snow was still falling heavily when Flight 90 eventually taxied into position and rumbled down the runway. The pilots adjusted the wing-flaps, raised the nose, and guided the plane off the runway and into the air, heading north in preparation for making a gentle left turn that banked towards the Potomac River. But while the nose of the plane pulled up sharply, it would not gain altitude. They were flying too low. Suddenly the aircraft shook violently, began to stall and started to plummet towards the 14th Street Bridge crossing the Potomac River. It was just after four o'clock and the bridge was packed with homebound commuter traffic.

With its nose up and tail down, Flight 90 slammed into the four-lane bridge, shearing off the top of one car and crushing four others, tearing off a huge section of bridge railing before it crashed into the icy Potomac. The plane broke up as it plunged to the bottom of the river. Only six people struggled from the submerged wreckage to the surface. They clung to a small section of the tail that remained afloat and waited for help to arrive.

It didn't take long. The first to arrive on the scene was a National Park Service helicopter, but as it circled the river there was almost nothing to see – just small pieces of floating wreckage bobbing among the jagged ice shattered by the impact of the crash. The Air Florida 737, a large commercial airliner, had disappeared. The helicopter crew located the six survivors clinging desperately to the tail, and the pilot manoeuvred the craft dangerously close to the black, cold water while they lowered a lifeline towards the victims. One of the first survivors to reach the lifeline was a man described as 'in his fifties, balding and with an extravagant moustache'. He immediately passed the lifeline to someone else, waiting while the helicopter ferried the victim to the safety of shore and turned around as quickly as possible.

By now a large crowd had gathered on the banks of the freezing river, ambulances and paramedics, as well as TV camera crews and helpless onlookers spellbound by the tragic drama unfolding in front of them. One of the helicopters reached a victim in a desperate plight, numbed by the cold and temporarily blinded by jet fuel spilt during the crash. Priscilla Tirado, a flight attendant, struggled to hold on to the lifeline, then she lost her grip and slipped and fell as the helicopter dragged her towards shore. She struggled for a moment and began to slip beneath the dark water. The helicopter circled frantically, but Ms Tirado was too exhausted to grab the lifeline again.

Suddenly, a man rushed from the crowd of onlookers. He dived into the icy river and, ignoring the deadly cold, he swam towards the drowning woman as she slipped beneath the ice. He frantically pulled her to the surface and struggled back towards the waiting medical crews on shore.

The drama was not quite over. When the helicopter returned for the man who'd passed the lifeline to the other victims, he was gone. He'd slipped quietly to his death in the frozen river and became known as 'the man in the water'. Later he was identified, and the 14th Street Bridge was renamed the Arland D. Williams, Jr. Memorial Bridge in his honour.

Less than two hours after Flight 90 took off from Washington National Airport, seventy-four passengers and crew were dead. There were only five survivors. Another five people had been killed on the 14th Street Bridge. The subsequent investigation found that Flight 90 crashed because the crew failed to turn on the anti-ice mechanisms, which meant that the engines filled up with ice and snow. There would never have been enough speed for lift-off.

The man who rescued Priscilla Tirado was 28-year-old Lenny Skutnik. TV footage of his heroic actions was replayed around the world, and President Reagan invited him to the White House and awarded him a medal for bravery. When Lenny Skutnik was interviewed, he explained that he didn't think he was a hero, and he wasn't even sure why he'd rushed into the river. He just

couldn't stand by and watch
the flight attendant
die. He was just
as surprised as
everyone else when
he rushed to rescue
the woman.

HEROES

Why did Lenny Skutnik risk his life to rescue Priscilla Tirado? Is it that remarkable?

Trained rescue workers such as helicopter crews, paramedics, police and firefighters will rush towards an emergency – that's what they've been trained to do. They will risk their lives to rescue people. Hundreds of police and firefighters rushed into the World Trade Center's twin towers in New York City after the terrorist attack on 11 September 2001, and hundreds of them died when the buildings collapsed. Thousands of volunteer firefighters risked their lives fighting huge bushfires ringing Sydney in the summer of 2001–2002. Some of them saved other people's properties while their own burned down. Other firefighters came from interstate, travelling long distances to help with the effort.

But Lenny Skutnik wasn't a trained rescue worker. He didn't even know Priscilla Tirado. His actions were truly altruistic: with no benefit to himself, he risked his own life to save a complete stranger.

ScratcHing Backs

People today still behave pretty much the same way as they behaved a century or a millennium ago. They are inspired by the same emotions and the same needs. People in ancient Greece or ancient China felt love and anger, empathy and hatred, jealousy and greed, just like us.

Recently, scientists have begun exploring 'evolutionary psychology' – psychology or behaviours that people have inherited from their ancestors. If it was only the biggest and meanest of our ancestors who'd managed to eat and have children, we should all be big and mean. When food is scarce, that nice person who waits their turn would be more likely to starve to death, so their genes and their tendency to be nice would not be passed on to the next generation. In evolutionary terms, nice behaviour selects for extinction.

Of course, a tribe of cooperative hunters could also do well – they'd plan the hunt together, work together in catching the prey, likely be more successful because they cooperated, and bring the food back to the cave to be shared among everyone. But this situation could be open to exploitation. A tribe member who was lazy and selfish wouldn't risk getting hurt out hunting, but would stay at home eating, ensuring his genes for the next generation. Pretty soon the tribe would be full of lazy, selfish, uncooperative genes.

Yet people do cooperate with each other, and they are nice to each other, most of the time. So what happened?

The most popular theory is 'you scratch my back, I'll scratch yours', or reciprocal altruism. Some of our ancestors learned to share food only with members of the tribe who shared with them. Thus they could cooperate without being exploited. The lazy guy who never brings back any food doesn't get fed. And it's not always your turn to go out for dinner; sometimes you get to laze around the fire and have a good time. It makes sense to cooperate with people who cooperate with you.

An Anarchist Utopia

A Russian prince proposed the theory of 'mutual aid' at the beginning of the twentieth century. Prince Peter Kropotkin conducted a scientific study of animals in Siberia – a very tough place to survive. He observed that not only were animals more likely to cooperate with each other than fight over scarce resources, but that people were too. He believed people were evolving into a society that would be non-political and cooperative.

Kropotkin was one of the last great anarchist thinkers. He proposed an ideal society where people would organise themselves into cooperative communes, and would share everything equally according to their need, because of the principle of mutual aid. It was a utopian vision and still influences anarchist philosophy today. But Prince Kropotkin's ideas got him into a lot of trouble. He was imprisoned for revolutionary activities in 1874, escaped to England, travelled to Switzerland where he was expelled, and shifted to France where he was imprisoned for three years. He lived in Britain until 1917, then returned to Moscow after the beginning of the Russian Revolution. He died in 1921 – the year before Stalin became General Secretary of the Communist party.

The prince did not live to see Stalin seize power and

enforce his policy of communal ownership of agriculture and industry – and the food shortages and famines and bloody purges that followed, that would see millions of people die.

HieRaRCHY oF Needs

In the middle of the twentieth century, a psychologist named Abraham Maslow proposed that a 'hierarchy of needs' also motivates an individual's behaviour.

The first need is food and water. A hungry or a thirsty person will think about little else than finding something to eat and drink. They're not particularly interested in philosophy or the stock market, or maybe even being nice to other people. But having satisfied the first need, people start thinking about the second need – shelter, a cave or a roof over their heads. People search for security. Having achieved a food supply and somewhere to live, their minds turn to the third need – love and a sense of belonging. Humans are social animals; they need to be with other people. Solitary confinement has always been regarded as a particularly cruel and drastic form of punishment. People need each other. We need to feel loved, we need a family and a community. The fourth need is esteem – not only do we want to belong to a family or community, but also we want to be liked and respected. Maslow also suggested a fifth need, self-actualisation – the need to understand the world, to create, or to solve problems just for the fun of it.

Maslow's hierarchy of needs helps explain both altruistic behaviour and barbaric behaviour in some situations.

AGGRESSiON aND TERRiTORY

An Austrian zoologist, Konrad Lorenz, was studying the behaviour of young birds when he discovered that ducklings would follow and attach themselves to the very first thing they saw when they hatched – usually the mother duck. Lorenz called this imprinting. When Lorenz substituted himself for the mother duck, the ducklings followed him everywhere. Konrad Lorenz was the founder of ethology, the study of animal behaviour.

Lorenz and other scientists became interested in what animals can tell us about the dark side of human nature. What makes people prone to violent and aggressive behaviour; why do people fight, murder and start wars?

In the mid-1960s, several books were published that caused a sensation. Robert Ardrey wrote about mankind's origins, proposing that man the hunter, man the killer rose out of Africa. He went on to write another book called *The Territorial Imperative*, and Konrad Lorenz published *On Aggression*, both proposing that aggressive behaviour is closely linked to matters of 'territory'.

When a male lion drives off the head of a pride and becomes the new dominant male, he will often kill all the cubs and mate with their mothers. This behaviour has also been observed in other animals such as baboons and gerbils.

Rats in a cage

A psychologist named John B. Calhoun performed a classic experiment with laboratory rats that demonstrated the territorial urge. He constructed a network of cages containing four pens, two with only one entrance which could be defended by a dominant male, and two in the middle which were very difficult to defend. Two dominant males (with a retinue of females) quickly established the desirable pens as their own territory, forcing the rest of the males to live in the central pens. The central pens became overcrowded and the rats fought constantly trying to establish a territory. As the overcrowding got worse, so did the rats' behaviour – they formed gangs and raped, killed and became cannibals.

In their natural state, rats have elaborate courtship rituals and rarely fight to the death. Overcrowding had induced anti-social or 'criminal' behaviour in the rats.

SEXY CHIMPANZEES

Evolutionary psychologists have been particularly interested in studying bonobos, a close cousin of the chimpanzee – they are only about 1.5 million years apart in evolutionary terms (which is not very long at all!). Bonobos are smaller than chimpanzees but otherwise look much the same. However, the two groups behave very differently. Males dominate chimpanzee bands, and social order is enforced with fighting and aggression. A new dominant male will sometimes kill all the babies and mate with the mothers.

Bonobos, on the other hand, are known as the 'sexy chimpanzee'. Bonobo bands are female-centred, and social tension is relieved with affection and sex – in fact, they'll have a quick orgy until everyone feels better. Bonobo bands are egalitarian and free from any serious violence.

One and a half million years of evolution separate fighting and war from free love and peace.

THE SELFISH GENE

A biologist named Richard Dawkins put forward a different theory to try to explain why people act the way they do. When he wrote *The Selfish Gene*, he proposed that most 'selfish' behaviour is designed to ensure the survival of the gene above that of the individual. The dominant male lion will only last a few years as head of the pride. In order for his genes to survive, the lion must ensure new baby lions carrying the same genes are under way as quickly as possible.

The 'selfish gene' theory can be explained in evolutionary terms something like this. The first life on Earth was created in the chemical soup of the primordial oceans when some amino acids discovered the trick of copying themselves. They became replicating molecules. It gave them a real edge: they survived and their non-copying relatives did not. Pretty soon, the replicating molecules dominated the oceans and learned new tricks to survive. They built little walls around themselves to protect them from the chemical warfare going on outside in the oceans, and the first cells were created.

Some of these cells learned to use the energy in sunlight to build more complex molecules. They would eventually evolve into plants. Others learned to consume each other, and would eventually evolve into animals. All of them would learn new tricks to survive and replicate. They'd grow branches and leaves, and fins and teeth. Some of them would be winners and go on to survive and replicate, and some of them would die out – the end of the line for their replicating molecules.

Although it was a tough battle, the replicating molecules were the real winners. Every cell of every animal and plant contains a complete set of replicating instructions inside their DNA. There are about a thousand million million cells making up the average human body. The design instructions for a complete human (you) are encoded inside every single cell of your body. Indeed, you began life as a single cell, and every single instruction for building your body was contained inside that cell. Every time the original cell divided to create a new cell, it took with it another complete set of instructions. In fact, the replicating molecules achieved a sort of immortality – when an original organism dies, the DNA lives on in its offspring.

SURVival MaCHines

Now stop and think about that. We are all, plants and animals alike, survival machines, built and designed by our replicating molecules for their survival, not ours. Our bodies control us, we do not control our bodies. Sure, you might be able to control whether you're fit or not, or whether you can hit a tennis ball, but you can't decide to grow a new arm – yet the original design for that arm is contained inside every single one of your cells. (There are a few special exceptions such as sperm and eggs, but they don't concern us here.) This is the theory behind cloning. Inserting the DNA from one of your cells into an egg which has had the original DNA removed gives that egg the potential to grow a whole new individual – a clone, a genetically exact copy of you.

Genes?

DNA is made up of very very long strings of nucleic acids. There are only four nucleic acids: C for cytosine, G for guanine, A for adenine and T for thymine. Genes are sections of DNA that carry inherited characteristics; for example, there is a gene that controls eye colour in people – the blue-eye or brown-eye gene. Genes are arranged on chromosomes, which are just separate strands of DNA found inside the centre, called the nucleus, of every cell. So the 'selfish gene' refers to inherited characteristics that help the gene to survive.

SO THE STORY GOES . . . GATTACA

The science-fiction movie GATTACA is set in a world in the not-too-distant future, a world ruled by genetics. Everybody's future is decided at birth by their genetic make-up. Babies with 'superior' genes are trained to be leaders and scientists and are given all the good jobs – they are the 'Valids'. The 'In-valids' are babies with 'inferior' genes, and they are trained to do all the lowly work.

Vincent is an In-valid with dreams of becoming an astronaut, which seem hopeless until he meets a Valid crippled by an accident who agrees to help. For a while, Vincent fools everyone and starts a successful career, and it looks like he's headed for the stars. But it could all come undone if his real genetic code is discovered. All his hard work, all his achievements, count for nothing if he doesn't have the right genes.

Sound crazy? In the not-too-distant future, health insurance companies might ask for genetic screening before they will insure you. If you have a gene for heart disease they might not give you medical insurance. Your genes might determine your future.

Of course, the title of the movie is based on a sequence of nucleic acids – G A T T A C A.

WOMEN AND CHILDREN FIRST?

So, what about Lenny Skutnik? Diving into a freezing river to save a complete stranger wasn't going to help his genes to survive. Now, if the drowning woman was a relative it would make some 'selfish gene' sense. By saving his daughter, he would also be saving a copy of his genes. Of course, the copy isn't exact – we aren't exactly the same as our parents, we aren't exactly the same as our brothers and sisters, or our uncles and aunts. We share half our genetic material with a parent, and in turn will contribute half our genetic material to our children – so they're carrying a lot of our genes. Using 'selfish gene' reasoning, the first person you save is yourself (exact copy of your genes). The next person would be a child or a parent, and after that a brother or sister, followed by uncles and aunts, cousins and so on.

Would you save your parent before your child? The selfish gene helps to explain that decision. If you're old enough to have a child, your parents are probably too old to have any more children. They aren't going to pass on any more genes – there's a better chance your children will. You save them first. Your partner, the other parent of your children? While you share no genes in common, you both share an interest in your children's survival, and they'd come pretty high on the list of who you'd save first.

What about brothers and sisters? Although you share a lot of genetic material, the 'selfish gene' sets siblings against each other. Each must fight to get more of their parents' care and attention so they have a better chance of growing up to survive and reproduce. Even baby birds squabble in a nest for the largest share of the food. If there are too many mouths to feed and not enough to eat, the stronger chicks will attack the weaklings and tip them out of the nest.

Me, MY Genes anD I

This could all be very depressing. It could be used to explain why people behave so selfishly: me and my genes' survival are all I'm interested in, and who cares about anyone else? But, throughout history, people like Lenny Skutnik have acted against their selfish genes' best interests and risked their lives to save others. Humans are social animals – we need to live in a community and feel loved and wanted. Perhaps it's the wider social bonds that motivate altruism, putting

I HOPE YOU APPRECIATE HOW MUCH I HAD TO BATTLE WITH MY GENETIC PREDISPOSITION TO SELFISHNESS IN ORDER TO GET YOU THIS.

other people before ourselves. People have the capacity to be more than their selfish genes; we can learn from the examples of others to stand up for what we think is right, and to display acts of kindness and generosity and courage. People like Lenny Skutnik are truly heroes.

Sinking the Titanic

On the night of 14 April 1912, the British luxury passenger ship *Titanic* hit an iceberg. Twenty minutes later, the ship sent out a distress signal, and within forty-five minutes the ship was listing to one side. The 'unsinkable' *Titanic* was sinking.

Passengers were initially reluctant to get into the lifeboats; surely the *Titanic* would stay afloat? When the first boat was launched, it left with only twenty-eight people, although it was capable of carrying sixty-five.

As the tilt on the deck grew steeper, passengers struggled to clamber into the lifeboats. The 'unsinkable' *Titanic* was not prepared for the eventuality that the entire ship would need to be evacuated, and there were not enough boats for everyone on board. There was widespread panic. Ship's officers tried to restrain people from jumping into the lifeboats from the rails. If the lifeboats were swamped or overturned, everyone in them would die. Lifeboats were filled with 'women and children first', and many men kissed their families goodbye, then remained on board, knowing they wouldn't survive. Amid the confusion, the managing director of the shipping line that built the *Titanic* managed to board a lifeboat, but there were more than 1000 people still left on the ship when the last boat pulled away. Ten minutes later the lights went out on the ship. Two minutes later the *Titanic* tilted almost perpendicularly to the water, broke up and quickly sank to the bottom of the ocean.

The survivors in the lifeboats could hear the screams and shouts for help from people drowning in the freezing water, but the cries didn't last for long. Less than an hour later the sea was utterly quiet. The *Titanic* was gone and nearly 1500 people were dead.

Two brave sailors had remained at their stations until almost the last moment – the radio operators who were sending frantic distress calls to any nearby ship. They did not survive, but their wireless plea for help had been heard, and in the early hours of the following morning, a ship finally arrived to rescue the survivors.

SO THE STORY GOES . . .
AND THE BAND PLAYED ON

There were eight musicians travelling on the *Titanic*, employed to entertain the passengers during its maiden voyage. After the initial collision with the iceberg, the band started playing music in the first-class lounge to help calm the passengers. As the ship began to tilt, they shifted onto the deck, and many survivors reported that the band kept playing while the ship went down. All eight musicians died.

There were many rich and famous people on board the *Titanic*. Mr Benjamin Guggenheim had made his fortune in the steel industry, and he had a reputation as a bit of a cad. He was travelling with his mistress. But within an hour of the collision, he and his personal secretary, Victor Giglio, took off their lifebelts and dressed in suits and hats. 'We are prepared to go down like gentlemen,' he explained. He asked for a message to be passed on to his wife in New York: 'I think there is grave doubt the men will get off. I am willing to remain and play the man's game

if there are not enough boats for more than the women and children. I won't die here like a beast. Tell my wife that I played the game out straight to the end. No woman shall be left aboard this ship because Ben Guggenheim was a coward.' Both Guggenheim and his secretary perished. His mistress survived.

Major Archibald Butt was an Ambassador and a close friend of the American President. He was playing cards in the First Class Smoking Room when the *Titanic* hit the iceberg. He escorted a female friend to a lifeboat and said, 'Goodbye, Miss Young. Luck is with you. Will you kindly remember me to all the folks back home?' He returned to the Smoking Room with his friends to resume their game of cards, and was seen by survivors in the lifeboats standing on the bridge as the ship went down.

SO THE STORY GOES ...
UNSINKABLE MOLLY BROWN

There were heroes in the lifeboats as well.

Molly Brown was in her cabin reading when suddenly something crashed overhead and threw her out of bed and onto the floor. The *Titanic* had just hit the iceberg. In the corridor, a man told her to grab a life-preserver and head for the deck, where she was quickly dropped into a lifeboat with fourteen women and one sailor. The sailor took a very dim view of their chances of survival, believing the lifeboat would be sucked under the water when the Titanic went down, and that they were all going to die. Molly grabbed an oar and ordered another young woman to help her row away from the sinking ship. She kept them rowing for several hours until a rescue ship appeared, and once on board the ship she helped organise the rescue effort and formed a committee of wealthy survivors to raise money for the destitute survivors. By the time they reached New York, she'd collected almost $10,000 (a lot of money at the time!). She went on to be known as the 'unsinkable Molly Brown'.

HEROES OF THE ANDES

On 12 October 1972, an aeroplane crashed into the side of a mountain in a remote area of the Andes. There were forty-five people aboard the chartered flight: a group of fifteen college boys scheduled to play in a series of rugby matches in Santiago in Chile, their friends and relatives, and a crew of five.

The mountain range is among the highest on earth, and the weather had been bad. When the plane descended through a blanket of clouds, the pilot realised they were flying too low and hadn't cleared the mountains. There was no time to do anything. The right wing clipped the side of the mountain and was torn off, somersaulting into the tail and slicing it off. Three of the boys and two crew members were instantly sucked out of the plane. A moment later the left wing was crushed, but amazingly the fuselage slid across the snow at 370 kilometres per hour before it came to a sudden halt. Several more people were missing, either hurled out of the plane or crushed during the crash, and others were critically injured. There was panic and hysteria. Two of the boys were medical students and they helped the survivors as best they could, but it was a terrible first night, alone on a snow-covered mountain some 3700 metres above sea level.

In the morning they decided they were lucky to be alive. While it was very cold and they didn't have much to eat, they could melt snow for water, and surely they'd be rescued soon. They made the fuselage as comfortable as they could, and they waited.

Eight days later they hooked up the plane's radio to a battery and heard that the search had been called off. Apparently the white fuselage was impossible to see against the snow. No one was coming; no one was going to rescue them. They were on their own.

The survivors improvised, using the plane's seat covers as blankets, and strapping chunks of aluminium from the wreckage to their feet as snowshoes. Insulation foamtorn from the plane was used as sleeping bags. A few chocolate bars, biscuits and wine were carefully rationed.

It was unbearably cold in the thin mountain air, they were scared and the food was starting to run out. But worse was still to come. On the sixteenth night, while everyone was asleep, an avalanche tore through the fuselage and suffocated another nine people. All the dead bodies were carried outside and buried in the snow.

By the twentieth day the survivors were starving. The dreaded topic was raised: the only food they had left was the frozen bodies. The medical students explained that if they didn't eat they also would die. After a lot of discussion and several more days without food, they cannibalised the dead, slicing off strips of flesh and eating it raw because there was no fuel for a fire.

When nearly six weeks had passed since the crash, they realised that no one was going to come to their rescue and they were going to die on the mountain. There was nothing left to lose, so two of the boys decided to try to hike out of the mountains. It was incredibly brave and risky, but ten days later they descended out of the snow and came across a shepherd. They told him their story, and within hours of their rescue, helicopters arrived at the crash site and brought out the remaining fourteen people still alive. In total they'd survived for seventy-two days.

Eventually the true story of their survival became known. No one wanted to believe it, but when the gruesome evidence of the mutilated bodies was discovered, the survivors reluctantly admitted they had resorted to cannibalism. The Chilean government decided to bury the bodies on the mountain where they'd died, and the fuselage was burned with the dead co-pilot still inside.

THE COURAGE TO SPEAK UP

'I disapprove of what you say, but I will defend to the death your right to say it.'

(Voltaire)

At the beginning of the eighteenth century, France was nearly bankrupt. There was widespread unemployment, poverty and misery. Not for the Royal Court and the aristocrats, though – they were extremely rich and having a great time. King Louis XIV was on the throne and he ruled by divine right, which meant he could pretty much do what he liked. The Church wasn't much help – the priests were generally corrupt, and didn't care what the aristocrats did as long as they followed the 'true faith'. People still believed in witches and sorcery, and anyone who questioned the Church's teachings could be charged with heresy, tortured, and burnt at the stake. The aristocrats treated ordinary people like slaves and playthings. Lawyers believed the law was designed to keep the people in their place. Doctors believed illness was a punishment from God, and if you got sick it was because you deserved it.

But change was in the air. The new natural scientists who were studying astronomy and mathematics began to believe that nature was subject to reason – that things had rational explanations rather than being the mysterious workings of God.

A young man born to a middle-class family in France began to question the world around him. Voltaire wrote about what he thought, in the form of witty satirical plays and essays ridiculing the ignorance of the rich and powerful. When Voltaire was twenty-four, his first play was produced in Paris. It was wildly successful and he became extremely famous. Luckily, his quick wit made him popular at court and the queen was very fond of him, but even so he was thrown into prison on several occasions and was only released because some of his powerful friends came to his help. He got into so much trouble on one occasion that he was only released from the Bastille (the main prison in Paris) on the promise that he would leave France and go and live in England.

That would prove to be a mistake for the aristocracy of France. In England, Voltaire was welcomed with open arms by the great thinkers of the day. Life wasn't so repressed in England, and when Voltaire returned to France, he was ready to try something new. Instead of appealing to the aristocrats to change their ways, he began writing for ordinary people. He wrote about how slavery was wrong. He argued that everyone should have the right to freedom of speech and the press, to live a life of liberty, and the right to work and own property. This was extremely radical at the time, and once again Voltaire was in trouble. He decided he should keep his head down and fled to a remote part of France, but eventually his fame spread throughout the world. Many years later he returned in triumph to Paris. During his life he made some provocative statements:

- 'If God did not exist, it would be necessary to invent him.'
- 'Work banishes those three great evils, boredom, vice and poverty.'
- 'History is just the portrayal of crimes and misfortunes.'

- 'One owes respect to the living; but to the dead one owes nothing but the truth.'

Voltaire died just a few years before the ordinary people of France decided they'd had enough.

THe FReNCH ARe ReVoLTiNG

In 1774, a new king, Louis XVI, ascended the throne of France. His queen, Marie Antoinette, was an Austrian princess. She was extremely unpopular, and on occasion she was hissed at and booed in the streets of Paris. She became involved in a scandal over a diamond necklace she was said to have ordered which was worth an enormous amount of money. It was rumoured that, when she was told that the poor people were starving and had no bread to eat, she replied, *'Qu'ils mangent de la brioche!'* ('Well, let them eat cake!') It probably wasn't true, but she was so unpopular that people were quick to believe it, and the nasty rumour spread.

The crops failed in France in 1788. There was widespread famine. People really were starving, and the peasants began to burn the houses of the rich aristocracy. There were rumours in Paris that the king had sent for the troops and intended to turn them loose on the people. In a Parisian café, someone leapt onto a table and declared they should storm the

Bastille, attack the soldiers and free all the prisoners. It seemed like a good idea. Quickly a mob surrounded the prison and did just that, releasing among other people the Marquis de Sade, the infamous aristocrat who had been jailed for offensive behaviour and whose name gave us the word 'sadist' (someone who enjoys inflicting pain).

OFF WiTH THeiR HeaDS

Eventually the king panicked, and he and the queen fled Paris. They intended to return with an army and put down the mob, but Louis and Marie Antoinette were captured by the revolutionaries and imprisoned in the Bastille. The king was tried, found guilty of treason, and guillotined in January 1793. Marie Antoinette followed him later in the year.

A rather nasty man was responsible for the queen's death. Maximilien Robespierre invented the slogan 'liberty, equality, fraternity', and suggested that the only way the revolution would succeed was if everyone who didn't agree was rounded up and executed. The 'Terror' began. More than 2600 suspects were executed in Paris alone, including scientists and poets and people who just thought all the mass murder was going a bit too far. As others took up Robespierre's ideas, children and even infants were sent to the guillotine. New and gruesome ways to kill people were explored. Children were shot and clubbed to death, 500 at a time in one incident. Prisoners were executed in mass drownings – hundreds were herded into boats that were towed into the middle of the river and sunk while men waited on the banks to hack to death anyone who tried to escape. Even the Marquis de Sade

3.7 million
BCE
Earliest
hominids

resigned his job with the revolutionaries, saying it was 'horrible and utterly inhuman'. Robespierre would not be stopped, indeed he stepped up the execution schedule, beheading 1300 people in Paris in just one month.

Finally it was too much for the citizens of Paris. In 1794, troops burst into the city hall and shot Robespierre in the face. Later the same day, he and nineteen of his followers went to the guillotine.

SO THE STORY GOES . . . DR JOSEPH GUILLOTIN

If it hadn't been for Louis XVI, the world might never have seen the invention named after Doctor Joseph Guillotin. Several years before the revolution, the king's physician was asked to look at a new 'humane' beheading machine.

Previously, only nobles were offered the quick and dignified death of beheading with a sword or axe. Ghastly methods of execution were in use for ordinary people: they faced torture with hot pincers, or their bones were broken on the wheel and the rack; they were slowly hung by the neck, or burnt alive at the stake. An even more terrible death was in store for anyone who attacked the king – to be hung, drawn and quartered.

PRIOR TO THE GUILLOTINE.

In 1757, a man lunged at Louis XV with a knife. Although the king wasn't badly hurt, the condemned man was tortured, and then his arms and legs were tied to four horses, which were driven in different directions in order to rip the victim's body into four pieces. After all this, the poor man was still alive, and finally he was hacked to death with a knife. Remember, executions were public, everyone saw what happened. They were appalled by the extreme cruelty of the execution.

With the coming of the Age of Enlightenment, it was decided a 'reasonable' method of execution should be devised. Dr Guillotin's radical suggestions included the proposition that everyone should face the same penalty, whether they were rich or poor. Criminals' families should not also be punished. Bodies of the executed person should not be mutilated and strung up for public display, and the method of punishment should be the same for everyone – decapitation and a quick, clean death.

Dr Guillotin was showing the king's physician the new invention when King Louis XVI wandered into the room. The king noticed they were having trouble with the blade and suggested an improvement – the cutting blade should slope rather than be curved. It was a success, and the guillotine was adopted as a reasonable and humane method of execution. Or so the story goes . . .

HOW LONG DOES A HEAD LIVE FOR?

Stories of decapitated heads trying to communicate emerged during the French Revolution. After the execution of Charlotte Corday, the executioner held up her severed head before the crowd and slapped her cheek. Spectators reported that her face reddened as though she was blushing. Other stories emerged, stories of decapitated heads blinking their eyes or their lips moving as they tried to speak. A debate raged about whether, and for how long, a severed head might survive being parted from its body.

Today, medical scientists believe a decapitated head might survive for as long as thirteen seconds – about as long as it takes for lack of oxygen to kill the brain – which is enough time for eyes to move and blink. But although the brain might be chemically 'alive', it is uncertain whether the victim remains conscious. The force of the blow might render the victim unconscious immediately ... or it might not. For thirteen seconds, the decapitated head may remain aware, still able to look around and observe the world.

YOU SAID IT WOULDN'T HURT!

THe FinaL SoLuTioN

Thousands of civilians died during the French Revolution. But it is estimated that more than forty *million* Europeans died during World War II. Five and a half million were Polish. Six million Jews were killed.

Jews were used as scapegoats when Adolf Hitler declared he had the 'Final Solution' for Germany's social and economic problems – remove all undesirable and racially inferior people in order to keep the German race 'pure'. These undesirables included Jews, gypsies, Slavs, mentally retarded people, the insane, the physically deformed and homosexuals, as well as political enemies.

Hitler came to power as the leader of the National Socialist (Nazi) party. At first, the Nazis passed laws to exclude Jews from many professions; later, Jews were encouraged to leave Germany. Finally, during World War II, Nazi policy was to have anyone of Jewish background killed. After Hitler had exterminated the Jews, he intended to wipe out the Slavs. Hitler considered this purification of race was essential if German people were to survive.

Hitler became obsessed with the 'Jewish problem'. He diverted trains to transport Jews to concentration camps rather than send desperately needed supplies to German troops fighting at the war front. He wanted every single Jewish man, woman and child dead – no one would escape, not even the old or the sick or newborn babies. Jews were rounded up and herded into trains and trucks to be shot, beaten, tortured, starved, hung, gassed and worked to death. It was terrible beyond belief. The number of dead was so great, it is easy to forget that each one of those deaths was murder. Somehow, the executioners found the stomach to murder again and again and again. They heard the people crying, the women and children screaming, pleading for their lives. They witnessed the piles of bodies, the blood, the broken bones and shattered skulls, the pain and suffering. Yet still they tortured and murdered.

Why did ordinary men and women turn into monsters? Very few of the executioners were in fear of their own lives: they made an active choice to be part of the Final Solution. No doubt many of them were convinced the women, children and babies they murdered were not humans deserving of care and sympathy, but mere things that needed to be eliminated.

A PRIEST WITH ATTITUDE

Not all Germans collaborated in the genocide. A German Christian pastor, Martin Niemoller, was imprisoned in a concentration camp for speaking out against the Nazis. He wrote a poem about how people's attitudes allowed the atrocity to happen.

When the Nazis came for the Communists
I was silent.
I wasn't a Communist.
When the Nazis came for the Social Democrats
I was silent.
I wasn't a social Democrat.
When the Nazis came for the Trade Unionists
I was silent.
I wasn't a Trade Unionist.
When the Nazis came for the Jews
I was silent.
I wasn't a Jew.
When the Nazis came for me
There was no one left
To protest.

SO THE STORY GOES . . .
THE COURAGE TO RESIST

Hitler was not content with making Germany racially 'pure' – he wanted to take over the rest of Europe as well. France was invaded by Germany in 1940, and with the German army came the Gestapo, the Nazi Party's secret police who used terrorism to stamp out all opposition and resistance. The Gestapo rounded up ordinary people, dragged them from their beds and took them away to be beaten, tortured and killed.

A young Australian woman named Nancy Wake was living in France at the time. As a journalist, Nancy had seen the brutality of the German stormtroopers in Vienna, where she had witnessed Jews being chained to a wheel

and beaten with whips. She decided she had to do everything she could to stop the Nazis. A few months after
the Germans occupied France, she joined the Resistance.

The Resistance movement in France consisted mainly
of young French people who opposed the German
occupation, and who were committed to driving the
occupiers out of France with any means available to
them. Nancy Wake was married to a wealthy Frenchman,
and she used her position as the beautiful wife of a rich
man to help smuggle refugees out of France, and to
carry messages and food to the underground Resistance
movement. She travelled on false papers and helped
more than a thousand escaped prisoners of war get out
of France safely, earning herself the nickname 'White
Mouse' in the process.

The Gestapo began to
suspect her. They tapped her
phone and opened her mail,
and by 1943 she was number
one on their 'most wanted'
list. It was too risky for
Nancy to stay in France,
and, after several
unsuccessful attempts,
she eventually reached the

safety of Britain. Her husband, also a Resistance worker,
stayed behind. It was not until the end of the war that
Nancy learned what had happened to him: a year after
she left, he was captured by the Gestapo and tortured
for information about his wife, and when he wouldn't
tell them anything, he was executed.

While she was in England, Nancy was trained by British Special Operations. She learned how to use guns and grenades, to kill silently, and to use explosives and radio codes. She parachuted back into France, where she helped supply weapons to the Resistance and organise sabotage raids against the Germans. It was a tough existence, constantly on the move, often living off the land and hiding in forests, always in danger. She and her comrades survived a concentrated attack by the elite Nazi soldiers, the feared SS, and Nancy personally led a raid on one Gestapo headquarters, killing a sentry with her bare hands before he could alert others to the raid. She shot her way out of roadblocks and executed a German female spy.

But Nancy always said that a bicycle ride was actually her most useful job. For seventy-one hours she cycled over 500 kilometres, alone and almost non-stop, through mountains and checkpoints, in constant fear and constant pain, to deliver new radio codes to other Resistance fighting groups.

Three hundred and seventy-five of the 469 British trained operatives working in France were alive at the end of the war. There were thirty-nine women operatives; the Germans killed twelve but another three managed to survive the torture and horrors of the Ravensbruck concentration camp. Nearly a quarter of a million French people died in prisons and concentration camps during World War II.

Un-AMERICan ACTIVITIES

Less than ten years after the end of World War II, an American senator found a new scapegoat – communists. Although America and the USSR were allies during the war, within a few years the arguments had begun and they were in the midst of a 'cold war' – a war with no open fighting but lots of mistrust, spying, propaganda and deception.

America believed that the spread of communism – the ownership of property and production by the state rather than individuals – had to be stopped. Senator Joseph McCarthy claimed to have a list of 250 government employees who were members of the Communist Party. Even when he was called before an investigating committee and had to admit there was no list, it didn't stop him. He used a smear campaign against people he suspected of being communists. He produced a list of 30,000 anti-American books written by communists and communist sympathisers and demanded they be removed from library shelves. He whipped up a witch-hunt of anti-communist hysteria, which would become known as 'McCarthyism'.

Senator McCarthy had help from the head of the Federal Bureau of Investigation (FBI), his friend J. Edgar Hoover. Hoover was convinced there was a communist conspiracy to overthrow the United States government. Over the years, the FBI had kept secret security files on just about everyone, and Hoover gave his friend access to this information. The files gave Senator McCarthy all the dirt he needed.

A committee was set up to investigate 'un-American activities', which included alcoholism and sexual deviancy as well as communism. Senator McCarthy questioned a lot of people in government departments about their political pasts. People lost their jobs if they admitted they'd ever been a member of the Communist Party. The only way to keep your job was to confess and name other people who were communist sympathisers or had left-wing views.

The House Un-American Activities Committee turned its attention to Hollywood. Senator McCarthy and J. Edgar Hoover were both convinced that communists had infiltrated the movie industry and the Screen Writers Guild:

> 'We are out to expose those elements that are insidiously trying to spread subversive propaganda, poison the minds of your children, distort the history of our country, and discredit Christianity . . . [There are] loathsome, filthy, insinuating un-American under-currents running through various pictures.'

Many members of the movie industry were called before the committee. Some left America to live overseas, and ten people refused to answer any questions at all. They became known as the Hollywood Ten and were found guilty of contempt of court and sentenced to between six and twelve months in prison. The investigation continued. Over 320 people were placed on a blacklist of suspected communist sympathisers. The list included musicians

Leonard Bernstein and Burl Ives, writers Lillian Hellman, Arthur Miller and Dorothy Parker, and actor/directors Charlie Chaplin and Orson Welles. Many of them also left the country and some never worked in America again. From 1947 to 1961, you couldn't get a job in Hollywood if your name appeared on that list.

It was several years before Senator McCarthy was finally discredited. By 1953 the committee's investigation was broadcast on prime-time TV, and when Senator McCarthy made some particularly nasty accusations to a witness, bullying the man until he broke down weeping and said 'Have you no decency, sir? Have you no decency?', it was the end for Senator McCarthy and the anti-communist witch-hunts. The mood of the public turned against him. Articles were published about McCarthy's own homosexuality. He lost his job. He began to drink heavily and died a few years later.

SO THE STORY GOES . . .
THE PRIVATE LIFE OF J. EDGAR HOOVER

J. Edgar Hoover was appointed Director of the Federal Bureau of Investigation in 1924, and was responsible for turning the agency into an efficient crime-fighting body. He recruited new staff and improved their training. He established a fingerprinting file in 1926 that would eventually become the largest in the world. He set up scientific crime-detection laboratories. He began to build up extensive secret files, and collected information about everyone from presidents to ordinary people. During the next decade, the FBI turned their attention to organised crime and arrested many major gangsters.

150,000 BCE
Homo sapiens evolve in Africa

After World War II, Hoover turned the power of the FBI on what he believed was a communist conspiracy, and even after Senator McCarthy was discredited, Hoover managed to keep his job. His secret files contained a lot of information about America's leading politicians, including incriminating material about their private lives that could destroy their careers. Hoover even accused Dr Martin Luther King of being 'the most notorious liar in the country'. J. Edgar Hoover served under eight presidents, and none of them was game to give him the sack. He died in his sleep aged seventy-two, while he was still the director of the FBI.

After Hoover's death, his private life became the subject of public scrutiny. All his life, Hoover had vilified and attacked homosexuals as sexual deviants, yet he himself had never dated a woman. His name was linked romantically with the assistant director of the FBI, Clyde Tolson. Both men were constant companions for over forty years; they ate lunch together, took holidays together, went out together, and went to work together every day. When Hoover died, Tolson arranged for Hoover's private files to be destroyed.

SO THE STORY GOES . . . BLACKLISTED

One of the Hollywood Ten was a screenwriter named Dalton Trumbo. He refused to name names and was sent to prison. After he was released, he discovered he had been blacklisted in Hollywood and couldn't get work. So Dalton Trumbo shifted to Mexico and continued to write under an assumed name. He wrote the screenplays for

Roman Holiday (1953) and *The Brave One* (1956), which, much to the embarrassment of the movie industry, both won Academy Awards for screenwriting.

It was 1960 before Dalton Trumbo wrote a screenplay under his own name again: that film was *Spartacus*, the true story of a slave rebellion in ancient Rome. At the end of the movie, the captured slaves are all crucified because they refuse to identify their leader, Spartacus, to the Roman general.

It was not until 1992 (sixteen years after he died) that Dalton Trumbo was finally credited under his own name with a posthumous Oscar for his original story for *Roman Holiday*.

SO THE STORY GOES . . . THE MALTESE FALCON

The man who wrote the famous American detective novel *The Maltese Falcon* was also swept up in the McCarthy hysteria.

As a young man, Dashiell Hammett had joined the army, and afterwards worked as a private detective for the Pinkerton Agency. He began to write crime stories and painted a new picture of an American society that could be greedy, treacherous and brutal. He created the tough private detective as a fictional character.

Hammett joined the Communist Party in the 1930s and became a fierce opponent of Nazism. After World War II, he continued to be involved in civil rights organisations, which Senator McCarthy and J. Edgar Hoover deemed to be subversive and un-American. Hammett was called before McCarthy's investigation but he also refused to name names, and in 1951 he was sentenced to prison for six months. After he was released, Dashiell Hammett was blacklisted. His books were taken off library shelves and the tax department claimed he owed a huge amount of money. He died penniless of lung cancer in 1961.

EVERYONE DOES IT

No political party or belief system has a monopoly on producing tyrants and tyrannical regimes. They are just as likely to come from the left of the political spectrum as they are from the right. Under the leadership of Joseph Stalin, the USSR undertook at least three 'purges', in which millions died.

The first was the deliberate famine in the Ukraine from 1930 to 1932. In 1929, Stalin ordered all farmland to be surrendered to the state. The independent farmers in the Ukraine (known as kulaks) ignored him, and Stalin decided to make an example of them, issuing the order to 'liquidate the kulaks as a class'. Stalin's secret police force, backed up by armed gangs, swept into the Ukraine and confiscated all property. Anyone who resisted was shot or clubbed to death, and those kulaks who survived were shipped to work camps in Siberia. When people began to fight back, Stalin sent in the USSR's regular forces, the Red Army, and by 1932 the Ukraine was in open warfare. Stalin demanded huge farm production quotas from the Ukraine, confiscating food and livestock and creating the largest man-made famine in history. While the people in the Ukraine were starving, the food they produced was being exported or left to rot. The people of the Ukraine capitulated.

70,000 BCE Homo sapiens reach south-east Asia

After the assassination of a popular Communist Party leader in 1935, Stalin became convinced he was surrounded by enemies. He began to purge his own Communist Party. Political leaders and army officers were shot. Thousands of innocent citizens were rounded up and shipped to Siberia. Then Stalin purged the purgers, and thousands of secret police were also killed. He purged the Red Army and sent most of the army leaders to prison, or had them killed. Finally, Stalin turned his attention to his citizens. Family members were encouraged to report on each other. Police and the secret police were themselves arrested if they didn't arrest enough citizens. At one time it was estimated that every fifth person was an informer.

More than one and a half million ordinary workers were arrested for subversive activities. On one night alone in 1937, Stalin approved 3167 death sentences. By 1938, at least five per cent of the entire population was under arrest. Estimates for the total number of dead range from twenty to sixty million people. More than eight million people were held in work camps. Stalin killed more Russian Army officers than died during World War II.

The purges ended suddenly in 1938, but when Hitler invaded the Soviet Union in 1941 on a thousand-mile front, the Red Army was incapable of mounting a defence and began to retreat back to Moscow. The USSR had the highest number of deaths during World War II – more

than 13.5 million military and more than 7 million civilians died.

One of the architects of Soviet communism had something to say about democracy:

> 'A democracy is a state which recognises the subjection of the minority to the majority, that is, an organisation for the systematic use of violence by one class against the other, by one part of the population against another.' (Lenin, *The State and the Revolution*, 1917)

Lenin died in 1924, three years before Stalin seized power.

I was just following orders

At the end of World War II, the Allies (the USA, Great Britain, France and the Soviet Union) prosecuted Nazi leaders for war crimes. Among the list of charges were murder, torture, enslavement, destruction of cities, towns, and villages, and the commission of crimes against humanity – the deportation and genocide of Jews and other groups in Europe.

The trial took place in the German city of Nuremberg. One defendant declared he could remember nothing of his Nazi past. Other defendants denied all knowledge of the horrors of the concentration camps. Some tried to blame everything on Hitler (who had committed suicide in the last days of the war). Others said they were just following orders.

The court was not convinced. The prosecutors produced documents that proved the defendants did know what was going on in the camps, and that they'd helped perpetrate crimes against humanity. The court decreed that 'I was just following orders' (which later became known as the 'Nuremberg defence') was not a proper defence. Eleven of the defendants were sentenced to hang, three to life in prison, and another four to years in prison. Three of the defendants were acquitted.

COUNTRIES WITH COURAGE

The Nazis had a master plan for exterminating all the Jews in Europe. Many countries actively assisted with identifying and rounding up (and sometimes killing) local Jews. A few countries did not.

Before the war, Denmark was a peaceful country of four million people. Many immigrants from surrounding countries lived happily side by side with the Danes, including Denmark's small Jewish population. People were proud of the fact that they all got along.

In 1940, Germany attacked and invaded Denmark. While most Danes were pro-British, they quickly realised they could not hope to keep the Germans out of their small country. So the Danes promised to supply agricultural and other products to the Germans, and in return the Danish government was allowed to continue to run the country. Within a year, the Danish Resistance movement began, and by 1943 the Danes had begun a campaign of sabotage.

The Nazis declared a state of emergency and finally decided to move against the Jews in Denmark. The deportation was to begin at 10 p.m. on 1 October 1943. The news leaked out two days before, and the Danes were outraged. The Danish people hid the Jews when the German soldiers came looking for them. They hid them in hospitals, they hid them in their homes, they gave them false papers and said they didn't know any Jews. The Danish police and coastguard refused to help locate and round up Jews. The whole country helped smuggle out Jewish refugees on small fishing ships. Only 481 Jews were captured and imprisoned, and constant pressure from the Danish government prevented them from being shipped to Auschwitz, the infamous death camp in Poland. The Danes sent supplies of clothing and food to the Danish Jews' camp, and insisted the Red Cross be allowed to inspect the prison's conditions. While the Nazis had estimated that more than five and a half thousand Jews lived in Denmark, it has been estimated that only sixty were killed during World War II. Not only did the Danes protect the Jews, but they also helped smuggle out allied airmen and other refugees fleeing from the Nazis.

After the war, as Jewish people returned to their homes across Europe, almost everywhere they discovered that their homes had been broken into, looted and destroyed. In some towns the returning Jews were actually attacked and killed. But not in Denmark. When the Jews returned, they discovered their neighbours had looked after their houses, their belongings, their gardens and even their pets.

30,000 BCE
—Neanderthals
extinct

The rescue of the Bulgarian Jews is another remarkable story of a whole country standing up for what they believed in. Forty-eight thousand Jews were estimated to live in Bulgaria at the start of World War II. The Bulgarians were allies of Germany, and the Germans insisted that the Bulgarian government should arrest all the Jews and deport them on trains to camps in other countries. At first the government agreed and ordered the Jews to be arrested, but the Bulgarian people were outraged when they heard what was happening. A lot of people protested. Farmers threatened to lie down on railway tracks to prevent the trains from leaving. Even the Bulgarian king, who came from a German family, was rumoured to have intervened. The government quickly released all the Jews. There were no Jews murdered in Bulgaria.

SO THE STORY GOES . . .
THEY RISKED THEIR LIVES

In other countries, it was individuals who found the courage to do what they thought was right, and sometimes the price was their life.

Father Jacques de Jesus ran a boys' school in Avon, France. He enrolled several Jewish students under false names and gave a noted Jewish botanist a job as a teacher. But Father Jacques was betrayed. The Gestapo arrived and arrested him, the Jewish students and the teacher and his family. The students and teacher all died at the infamous concentration camp at Auschwitz, and while Father Jacques survived in the camps until the end of the war, he had been treated so badly he died a few weeks later.

20,000 BCE
Sophisticated
cave art in
France

SO THE STORY GOES . . .
A HERO WHO COULDN'T FOLLOW ORDERS

A lot of people moved around Europe during World War II. Some of them were captured soldiers held in Prisoner of War (POW) camps; others were ordinary people relocated against their will (such as the Jews or forced labour workers) or refugees fleeing the horrors of the war. At the end of the war, all these displaced people had to be sent home.

In Italy, a British soldier was assigned to assist with collecting ex-Soviet soldiers and refugees and sending them back to Russia. Major Denis Hills faced an awful moral dilemma. Not only did he know a lot about eastern European countries and could speak several of the languages, but he had also sailed on the first ship to take 5000 ex-Soviet soldiers back to Odessa in Russia. What he saw in Odessa convinced him the men had been shot not long after they arrived.

Back in Italy he was placed in charge of a POW camp and ordered to send more Russians back home. What should he do? If he followed his orders he was sending men to their certain deaths; if he refused to obey orders he was committing treason.

Major Hills came up with an idea. He wasn't very good at running the POW camp; in fact, he was terrible. He left the gates unlocked at night (lots of prisoners just walked out the door). He invented new categories for the prisoners so they didn't have to be sent home. Finally, less than 200 prisoners remained, and he told them the truth as they left: 'You are the sacrifice. Because of you the others will be safe.'

It was not the only time Major Denis Hills chose to follow his conscience rather than his orders. At the end of the war, a shipload of Jewish refugees wanted to sail from La Spezia in Italy to Palestine. At that time, Jewish refugees wanting to travel to Palestine were deemed to be illegal immigrants, and on several occasions the British Navy refused to let them sail, even firing on the ships, boarding them, and in some cases returning the refugees to 'displaced person' camps. (Many of the refugees had already survived the horror of Nazi concentration camps.) At La Spezia, the refugees began a hunger strike and threatened to set the ship on fire, and the local Italians also wanted the refugees to leave. Eventually the British permitted the ship to sail under the escort of a British naval vessel. Major Denis Hills was the man who allowed the ship to leave.

HERO DOES CARTWHEELS

The British Army did catch up with Major Denis Hills eventually. Early one morning, he was seen turning cartwheels and handsprings in the main square of Trieste in Italy. He was court-martialled, reprimanded and demoted for behaving in an undignified way.

YOU ARE CHARGED WITH EXCESSIVE JUBILATION. HOW DO YOU PLEAD?

YIPPEE!

9000 BCE
Humans arrive in Americas

ASKING THE
RIGHT
QUESTIONS

THE BIG QUESTIONS.

9000-8000
BCE
Domesticated
animals &
crops in
Middle East

PHILOSOPHER DRINKS POISON

You can get into a lot of trouble by asking questions. Sometimes thinking for yourself can even prove to be fatal. Just ask Socrates – nearly two and a half thousand years ago he was sentenced to death because he refused to stop asking questions.

Socrates lived in Athens in ancient Greece. We know very little about his childhood, though history tells us he was particularly ugly with a potbelly, bulging eyes and a snub nose. Even when Socrates was a young man he was renowned for thinking. Once he stood in the same spot for hours thinking about a problem, and eventually people began to notice Socrates hadn't moved all day. A crowd of curious people gathered about him. As the sun began to set, Socrates was still deep in thought. A few people went home and brought back their sleeping mats, intending to stay and watch what would happen. Socrates continued thinking throughout the night, and when the sun finally rose, he muttered to himself and walked away, totally unaware of his spectators, who never did find out what he'd been thinking about!

Socrates was never rich, but his fame as a wise man grew until many influential people believed he was the wisest man in all Athens. Socrates argued with them: he believed that the more he learned, the less he realised he knew. Finally one of Socrates' rich friends declared he would settle the argument once and for all – he would ask the Oracle at Delphi.

The ancient Greeks believed the gods were responsible for everything that happened in the world. The gods controlled the weather, the success or failure of crops, sickness and health, the outcome of a battle. The temple

6500 BCE
Farming
in Greece

at Delphi was built to honour the Greek god Apollo, the god of sun, music, poetry and prophecy – and people came from far and wide to ask advice about the future and their fate. Over the entrance to the temple were carved the words 'Know Thyself!' Inside the temple a priestess sat on a stool situated over a fissure in the earth. Today we know the fissure emitted hypnotic natural gases that sent the priestess into a trance, but in ancient Greece people believed she spoke with the voice of Apollo when she answered their questions. Many rich and important people consulted the Oracle, as the priestess was known.

When Socrates' friend asked the Oracle if the philosopher was the wisest man in Athens, without hesitation she replied that he was. Socrates' friend returned in triumph to Athens with the news, but Socrates still wasn't convinced. He could think of many people who knew more than he did. The philosopher rushed off to talk to the wisest man he knew and proceeded to ask him questions about everything. Socrates was not totally satisfied with his answers, so the philosopher started asking other people questions. Every day he roamed the marketplace and streets of Athens and stopped everyone, rich and poor alike, to ask them questions about what they knew and what they thought and what they believed. He asked questions about everything. He even asked big, difficult questions such as: What is justice? What is truth? What is right and what is wrong? This upset a lot of important people in ancient Athens. They didn't like being questioned and they particularly didn't like it when their answers made them sound stupid. They became convinced that Socrates was a troublemaker and something should be done to stop him.

Of course, other people flocked to listen to Socrates. They believed he truly was a wise man, and that by listening to him talk they could learn how to think and maybe also become wise. Young men in particular came from far and wide to learn from Socrates, and they followed him around the markets and streets, stopping on corners and in doorways to listen to what he had to say. They began to ask questions too. They began to think for themselves. By the time Socrates was an old man, he was still very poor. He taught his students free, he didn't wear shoes in winter or summer and rarely washed his clothes. He didn't care about riches or money – he thought the freedom to think was more important.

Finally something was done about the 'troublemaker'. Socrates was charged with heresy and corrupting the young men of Athens. These were serious charges. Socrates was brought to trial before 500 of the most important people in Athens. He was found guilty of the charges by a narrow margin and sentenced to death. Socrates' friends advised him to flee the city, but he refused. He loved Athens and his search for truth, and he would not run away.

It was the custom at the time for condemned prisoners to drink poison made from hemlock. After a bath, and in the presence of some of his friends, Socrates took the cup from his jailer and drank the hemlock. He walked around for a little while until his legs became numb. Then he lay down and, a short while later, one of the greatest philosophers in history was dead.

Socrates never wrote anything down. It was only because one of the young men who followed him around the marketplace wrote about Socrates that we know so much about him today. That young man went on to become another very famous philosopher – he was Plato, the second of the great ancient thinkers.

DEATH BY POISON

Hemlock is a plant reaching about two metres high with small white flowers. The whole plant, especially the berries and roots, is poisonous. The prepared poison is usually ingested and causes paralysis of the nervous system – a sensation of numbness – followed by heart failure or cessation of breathing, symptoms similar to those of suffocation.

Using poison to murder people has a long tradition. Another popular poison from ancient Rome was cyanide, which can be extracted from laurel leaves. Cyanide is a quick-acting poison that works in much the same way as carbon monoxide – it starves the blood of oxygen. One of the signs of cyanide poisoning is a smell of bitter almonds in the victim's mouth or stomach contents. Oddly enough, the ability to smell cyanide is genetic: some people can smell it and others cannot. It was rumoured that Livia, the wife of the Roman emperor Augustus, soaked figs in cyanide before she fed them to her husband.

The Romans did not regard death by poison as necessarily a bad thing. Pliny the Elder, an ancient historian, believed that poison could relieve men of the burden of living when life became unbearable.

3500 BCE
Earliest city
in China

3100 BCE
Egypt is
united

3100 BCE
Writing
invented in
Middle East

3000 BCE
Farming in
Central
Africa

A PHILOSOPHER?

If you look in the dictionary, a philosopher is defined as a seeker after wisdom, a person who lives their life by the light of philosophy, or one who shows philosophical calm in trying circumstances. So, a philosopher is a person seeking wisdom, a person who lives their life according to that wisdom, and faces difficulties calmly with the help of those principles.

NATURAL PHILOSOPHERS

Socrates was not the first philosopher. The very first philosophers were interested in how the world worked. At that time, people usually explained the world in terms of gods and myths. People got sick because they offended the gods; crops failed because a magic ritual wasn't performed correctly. It was all beyond people's control and understanding. But some people began to observe the world around them and think about what they saw. Where did things come from? What made an egg hatch into a bird? How did things change? They were the first natural philosophers.

Some philosophers thought everything must come from water, while others thought it might be air, or a mixture of both. The ancient Greek natural philosophers finally agreed that there must be four elements: fire, water, air and earth; and that everything is just a mixture of these elements.

One of the last great natural philosophers was a man called Democritus. He took this idea one stage further,

2590 BCE
Great
Pyramid
built in
Egypt

2000 BCE
Stonehenge
built

2000 BCE
Minoan
civilisation
in Crete

2000 BCE
First metal-
working in
Peru

2000 BCE
Settlement
of Pacific
begins

believing that everything could be broken down into tiny particles that were the building blocks of everything. He called them atoms. Sound familiar? It was not until modern times that scientists began to agree with Democritus. Since then, scientists have gone on to split the atom and discover that there are still smaller elemental particles inside the atom – protons, neutrons and electrons. And even these can be broken down further. Modern physicists believe there will eventually be a limit beyond which they can go no further, and that then they will have discovered the very substance of the universe.

THE PHILOSOPHER'S LIFE

One of Socrates most famous quotes is:

'The unexamined life is not worth living.'

Socrates thought the most important thing in life was to think about who we are and what we are doing, to constantly examine our actions and ourselves, and to ask: What is the right thing to do? First we must carefully examine the question, and, having decided what is right,

1500 BCE
Writing in
China

1300 BCE
Fiji is
settled

1200 BCE
Beginning
of Jewish
religion

1150 BCE
Olmec
civilisation
begins

we need the courage to stand by our principles. Is it right to treat all people the same? If you decide that it is, you should try and live your life by that principle – you should treat everyone you meet, whether they are rich or poor, young or old, male or female, black or white, in exactly the same way. Just a minute, what about standing up for old people on buses and offering them a seat? Is it still right to treat them the same way? Old people get tired. They need to sit down. Hmm. You might like to modify your position. Is it right to treat all people the way I'd like to be treated? Then you could stand up for old people on buses and still live by your principles. What about little kids, or poor people who don't have the bus fare? By examining these questions we are using the Socratic method. It still works today. And you don't need a university degree to use it – everyone can be a philosopher.

DANGEROUS IDEAS

So what made Socrates so dangerous? He was a poor old man, hardly a real threat to the important people of Athens.

It was his ideas that made him dangerous. He was teaching young men how to think for themselves; that, rather than take things for granted, they should ask questions. Their elders and betters didn't like that idea. They were important people and believed everyone should listen to them and do what they said just because they were in charge. They didn't want things to change. They didn't want people asking questions and thinking for themselves.

Unfortunately for them, getting rid of Socrates didn't stop his ideas. They could kill the man, but not his philosophy.

PHILOSOPHERS RULE!

Socrates' pupil Plato was a young man when the old philosopher was sentenced to death. It affected him greatly. He was determined to tell the world about Socrates and he wrote books about what Socrates said and did.

Unlike Socrates, Plato came from a wealthy family and was destined for a career in politics. Later in life, his mind turned to other questions, about how governments should work, and how politics could be based on justice and reason rather than self-interest. He left Athens and travelled through the ancient world, including North Africa and Egypt where it was rumoured he was initiated into the mysteries of the ancient Egyptian priests.

Some of Plato's ideas were extremely radical for the time – he advocated the equality of the sexes and admitted women to his classes. Otherwise, Plato was a bit disillusioned with people, whom he thought often did foolish things (such as condemning Socrates to death). Plato didn't particularly believe in democracy:

'a charming form of government, full of variety and disorder, and dispensing a sort of equality to equals and unequals alike.'

Plato thought a Philosopher King should rule – a man who was wiser than ordinary citizens:

'There will be no end to the troubles of the states, or indeed . . . of humanity itself, till philosophers become kings in this world, or till those we now call kings and rulers really and truly become philosophers.'

Although Plato thought Greek citizens shouldn't be enslaved, he never questioned the institution of slavery.

Eventually Plato settled down and opened the first university. Plato's Academy was founded in 380 BCE, and finally closed by the order of the Christian emperor Justinian more than nine hundred years later in 529 CE.

There was a student at Plato's Academy, another young man in search of truth and wisdom, who would also become a famous philosopher. But while Socrates had questioned men, Aristotle would question things. He was a collector: of manuscripts, of geological and marine specimens, of vegetables and animals, the names of past rulers, a list of all the Olympic winners – he collected and studied and classified just about everything he could.

First he divided the world into living and non-living things, and the living things into humans and other creatures. He thought that by examining the world around him and using the power of logic (deductive reasoning) he could explain how things worked and how they were connected. He was the first modern scientist.

Of course, like his predecessors, he dabbled in politics, and finally had to leave Athens in a hurry when the

776 BCE
First
Olympic
Games in
Greece

political situation got too hot. Aristotle denounced absolute monarchies (kings) and oligarchies (a small group of rulers) as being interested only in themselves; and he denounced democracy as a form of tyranny by the masses – mob rule! He believed some people were born to be slaves and saw nothing wrong with slavery. He also did not share Plato's enlightened view of women: he thought women were 'unfinished men'. He even believed that babies existed in a tiny form inside a man's sperm, and that a woman was no more than a fertile field for a man to plant his seed in.

Unfortunately, in the Middle Ages, the Christian Church rediscovered Aristotle and agreed with his view of women.

Alexander the Great

Aristotle had his chance to influence a great ruler when he accepted a job teaching the young son of King Philip of Macedon. Aristotle couldn't have known that his new pupil would grow up to be the most powerful and famous man of the time.

The young prince's lessons were cut short; before Alexander was twenty years old, his father was assassinated and he suddenly became king.

'ALEXANDER THE GRATING' MORE LIKE IT.

650 BCE
Iron technology in China

600 BCE
First coins used in Greece

Aristotle returned quietly to Athens and Alexander went on to become Alexander the Great.

History records almost nothing about the relationship between Aristotle and his pupil, but Alexander did give instructions that all interesting biological and geological specimens collected during his many military campaigns were to be sent to his old teacher.

SO THE STORY GOES . . . A TRICKY KNOT

A short while after Alexander became king and began conquering other countries, he came to the kingdom of Phrygia, where the local king presented him with a knotty problem. A rope was tied up with a huge and complicated knot, and, legend had it, the Gordian knot could only be unravelled by the future conqueror of all Asia. Alexander considered the problem, and everybody held their breath, waiting to see what would happen. Alexander simply lifted his sword and sliced the knot in half.

He went on to conquer the known world.

ALEXANDER WEARS TROUSERS

A brilliant (and lucky) general, Alexander conquered Greece and Egypt, where he founded a new city he named after himself – Alexandria. He defeated the Persians and led his army into the north of India. And all of this was before he was thirty years old! His career was cut short a

couple of years later when he
suddenly fell sick and died. His
generals divided up Alexander's
empire and started to call themselves kings. A general called Ptolemy
controlled Egypt and founded a royal dynasty
that would finally end with Queen Cleopatra.

I SHALL NAME THIS
CONQUERED CITY
AFTER MYSELF!
I SHALL CALL
IT 'ME'.

Now, not everyone thought Alexander was
all that great. He settled Greek colonies in the
countries he conquered and tried to force Greek
culture on the people. He forced his generals and soldiers
to marry local women and settle down. He adopted
Persian customs and even wore trousers, considered by
the ancient Greeks (who wore short frocks and cloaks) to
be a most suspicious form of dress, a bit girlie in fact.

Even today, Alexander the Great is criticised by many
historians. Sometimes Alexander behaved like a mega-
lomaniac – he could be brutal, and he demanded absolute
loyalty – and after he conquered his extensive empire he
was unable to control it. We know today that one of the
most foolish manoeuvres an army can make is to over-
extend its lines. It's difficult to transport supplies over
long distances, or to send help quickly, and the more
soldiers that are left behind to make sure the local
populace behaves itself, the smaller and weaker the army
becomes. But, in Alexander's defence, he didn't have the
wisdom of hindsight – he was the very first person in
recorded history to conquer such a large area, and
couldn't anticipate the problems of governing and
administrating an empire. While Alexander did force
Greek culture onto other countries in the belief that he
was bringing civilisation to the barbarians, at least he

468 BCE
Death of
Siddhartha
Guatama

479 BCE
Death of
Confucius

399 BCE
Death of
Socrates

wasn't just looting and burning (as most armies did in those days). And don't forget, Alexander the Great died not long after he turned thirty. Who knows what he might have done if he had lived longer? It was a short and interesting life.

PHILOSOPHER LIVES IN A BARREL

Among the many philosophers who lived in ancient Athens were a group who followed the 'Cynic' school of philosophy. They believed that material things could not make you happy, and that true happiness could only be achieved by not needing things.

A Cynic called Diogenes gave away everything he owned except for a cloak, a cup and a walking stick. He was said to live in a barrel, and eventually he even gave his cup away

I HAVE GIVEN AWAY EVERYTHING I OWN EXCEPT FOR THIS CLOAK, THIS CUP, THIS WALKING STICK, THIS TELEVISION & PLAYSTATION, AND THIS SPORTS CAR.

when he saw a poor man drink from his hands. One day, Alexander the Great stood before Diogenes and asked if there was anything he wanted. 'Yes,' Diogenes said. 'Shift to one side, you're blocking my sun.'

380 BCE
Plato
founds
Academy

347 BCE
Death of
Plato

334 BCE
Alexander
the Great
begins
conquests

323 BCE
Death of
Alexander

322 BCE
Death of
Aristotle

ReVISITING HISTORY

How we see history is continually changing. During the building of the British Empire in the eighteenth and nineteenth centuries, historical figures such as Alexander the Great were considered heroic, and fine examples of how to behave. Today, when there are no more empires to conquer, he seems less relevant. We are more interested in how ordinary people were affected by events, by what caused the situation and what happened afterwards – by the big picture. No doubt as we change, the way we see the world will also change.

DIFFERENT WAYS OF SEEING.

THE LEGENDARY CONQUERING HERO, ALEXANDER THE GREAT, ON A HORSE.

A STRONG, BRAVE & COURAGEOUS HORSE, CARRYING A MAN.

THE KNOWN WORLD?

Of course there was a world outside Greece and the Mediterranean. Remember, at the time of the great philosophers, Greeks were writing most of the history, so it's forgivable and entirely understandable that they wrote about themselves and placed Greece at the centre of the world. But what was happening elsewhere in the philosophical world?

214 BCE
Great Wall
of China
built

202 BCE
Han dynasty
reunites China

THE ENLIGHTENED ONE

Northern India was divided into numerous small kingdoms with an increasingly complex caste system that categorised people into four major groups: the ruling elite, the warriors, the peasants, and servants. A fifth caste rapidly developed, the outcasts, or 'untouchables' – they did the jobs no one else would do, such as cleaning up toilets and handling dead things.

In about 563 BCE, an Indian prince was born who, at the age of twenty-nine, was so distressed by the suffering of the people around him that he turned his back on royal luxury. For six years, Prince Siddhartha Gautama lived an austere life as a wandering hermit and monk. Finally one day, while sitting under a bo tree (a type of wild fig), he realised that both extremes of living weren't the answer – it was the middle way that held the key. He became the Buddha, which means 'the enlightened one', and he went on to found one of the world's great religions – Buddhism.

The Buddha adopted a life of meditation, chastity, non-violence and poverty. He believed that all life was suffering, that all suffering comes from desire, and that to end suffering one must end desire. He taught people to have compassion, tolerance and respect for all forms of life. Anyone could end the suffering of life and continual reincarnation, he said, by meditating and living a virtuous and moderate life.

TAOISM

At about the same time that Prince Siddhartha was teaching, and nearly a century before Socrates would be born, legend tells of a philosopher in China who saw the corruption and evil around him and became sick at heart at how wicked people were. He abandoned his good job as a civil servant and went off alone, intending to die in the desert, but he was persuaded by a gatekeeper in north-western China to write down his teachings before he did.

Lao-Tzu wrote eighty-one short parables that became known as the *Tao-Te-Ching*, which would influence Chinese thought and culture for the next 2500 years, and eventually travel to the rest of the world. The Tao (the 'way') is to live a virtuous life and empty oneself of all worldly desires through silence and tranquillity.

These similarities with Buddhism helped Siddhartha's teaching gain acceptance in China a few centuries later, where Buddhism rapidly spread through the country and on to Korea and Japan.

CHiNESE PHiLOSOPHY

Another Chinese philosopher was also tackling the problem of how a good man could live in a wicked world. Confucius developed an ethical code, a way for people to live that was based on correct behaviour and respect. He thought good government (rather than force) was the best way to relieve the suffering of the poor, and – even more radical – that ordinary people could live up to high expectations. Confucius's philosophy became so influential in China that the civil service examinations were opened to everyone, and even a poor young man could obtain a high office and a good job through hard work and study.

A Few Contemporary Good Men

Philosophical arguments have continued up to and including the present day. In every era of history there have always been a few good men who have thought about what is wrong and what is right, and have been prepared to speak up for what they believe in.

At the beginning of the twentieth century, India was a British colony, but the British government was having problems – the Indians wanted their independence. The British government didn't want to give up the revenue from such a rich country, so they began to divide India into states, hoping that by dividing they could also conquer.

A new leader appeared on the scene to unite the country. Mohandas Gandhi led the struggle for Indian independence, but he was also a pacifist and didn't believe in violence.

> 'My notion of democracy is that under it the weakest should have the same opportunities as the strongest. This can never happen except through non-violence.'

Gandhi began a campaign of non-violent protest which was to prove extremely embarrassing for the British government. He organised strikes and staged the first 'sit-ins'. He was imprisoned several times, but he would not give up. People began to call him the Mahatma, which in Sanskrit (an ancient Indian language) means a 'great soul'.

Now, all this was happening while the Indians fought a bloody civil war between Hindus and Muslims that killed millions of people. During a terrible riot, a Hindu man came to Gandhi and cried, 'I have killed a child, a Muslim. How can I ever be forgiven?' And Gandhi told him he must take an orphaned Muslim child into his house and love him as his own son.

In 1947, India did achieve its independence from Britain, but, as with all the great thinkers, not everyone agreed with Gandhi, and the Mahatma was assassinated a year later by a Hindu nationalist.

Nelson Mandela

In 1948, the South African government passed new racial-segregation laws making everyone except white people second-class citizens. This apartheid meant that blacks and 'coloured' people couldn't attend 'white' schools, or use 'white' buses, or 'white' restaurants, or even live in 'white' streets.

SOUTH AFRICAN
PIANO — c.1960

A young black South African lawyer thought this was wrong, so he helped organise a political party, the African National Congress, to pressure the government for change. He was jailed for life in 1964 for plotting to overthrow the government. During his trial Nelson Mandela declared:

30 CE
Death of
Jesus of
Nazareth

'Whites tend to regard Africans as a separate breed. They do not look upon them as people with families of their own: they do not realise that they have emotions—that they fall in love like white people do; that they want to be with their wives and children like white people want to be with theirs; that they want to earn enough money to support their families properly; to feed and clothe them and send them to school. And what 'house-boy' or 'garden-boy' or labourer can ever hope to do this?'

Nelson Mandela spent the next twenty-six years of his life in jail. Even behind bars and living under terrible conditions, he still fought for justice and equality for all South Africans. He was finally released in 1990. The apartheid laws were changed, and in 1994 he became the first democratically elected South African president. He won the Nobel Peace Prize in 1993.

THE Consolation of PHILOSOPHY

Many centuries after the ancient Greek philosophers lived and died, a Roman politician was sentenced to death on unjust (and probably false) charges. Boethius wrote a book while he was imprisoned, a book of noble thoughts and great beauty. He called it *The Consolation of Philosophy*. Even today, if someone faces their problems with calmness and courage, we say they have 'taken it philosophically'. They have not angrily turned on the world or other people and blamed them; instead they have seen the big picture, what they can control and what they cannot, what is important in the world and what is not.

43 CE
Rome
invades
Britain

THE PHILOSOPHICAL MAN.

It's a bit like this – bad stuff happens to everyone. You get sick, you break your leg, you get caught in the rain, you miss the last bus, and once these things have happened there's not much you can do about them. Sure, you can get angry and yell at people, but that won't change anything. All you can change is the way you feel about it, how you react. There'll be another bus, or you can walk home. You can laugh about getting wet. Is it really important? As a popular modern piece of philosophy explains, no man on his deathbed has ever wished he'd spent more time in the office.

SO THE STORY GOES...
PHILOSOPHICAL DEATH

The Australian bushranger Ned Kelly showed a philosophical calmness on the gallows. His last words were reportedly, 'Such is life,' and he shrugged before they placed the noose around his neck. Ned Kelly went calmly and courageously to his own death.

BLOWING THE WHISTLE

Of course, living a philosophical life is not without its problems. Everyone at some time stops and thinks about the big questions: Who am I? Why am I here? This leads to other questions such as: What sort of person am I? What is the right thing to do?

If you live by philosophical principles, sometimes you must find the courage to stand up for what is right. It takes a lot of courage to be a whistleblower, a person who, generally with inside knowledge, sees that something is wrong and won't lie or keep quiet about it. They blow the whistle on corruption and cheating, whether it be falsifying scientific results or taking bribes, often at great personal cost.

One of the most famous modern whistleblowers was a New York police detective, Frank Serpico. He was a brave and honest man, but he had entered the New York Police Department (NYPD) in 1960 at a time when police corruption was entrenched. Police regularly took bribes to look the other way, and they were paid to warn criminals they were about to be arrested.

Frank Serpico was shocked. He refused to take money, and his fellow officers were immediately suspicious, but Serpico believed it was too important to ignore. He blew the whistle on the NYPD's corrupt activities and testified in court against a former partner.

Serpico received death threats. Finally he was shot in the face at point-blank range while making a drug bust. It was a set-up. Although Frank Serpico was seriously wounded, the other police officers at the scene did not call for help. Serpico survived the shooting and testified against the corrupt police officers. The NYPD was cleaned up. Serpico was awarded a Medal of Honour for conspicuous bravery and action, but his life was still in danger and he was placed on a witness protection program. He now lives back in New York.

150 CE Buddhism reaches China

165 CE Smallpox ravages Rome

POWER CORRUPTS

The world is full of temptations. A famous historian, Lord Acton, once wrote:

> 'Power tends to corrupt, and absolute power corrupts absolutely.'

Power and money can bring us lots of nice things. If you're rich and famous, people treat you with respect or at least deference. You can always get a good seat at a restaurant. You can afford a nice car, holidays, lots of stuff. Would you tell a lie for such a good life? Would you cheat? Would you kill? Start a war? The bigger the rewards, the bigger the temptation to bend the rules in order to keep those rewards. Maybe just a little lie... maybe I'll just take a little bribe, or look the other way when someone else does. People who have thought about the big questions, about who they are and what is right and what is wrong, often find these temptations easier to resist. Frank Serpico did.

THE EMPEROR'S NEW CLOTHES

Power, fame and money can also corrupt the people around you. People treat you differently because you're rich and important.

In the story of 'The Emperor's New Clothes' by Hans Christian Andersen, a tailor tells the emperor he will stitch a special set of clothes that can only be seen by intelligent people with great taste. In fact, there are no clothes – the tailor makes imaginary stitches in the air –

but the emperor is not game to admit that he can't see his new outfit, in case people think he is unintelligent and has really bad taste.

Not a single person in the empire has the courage to tell the emperor the truth. No one is game to admit that they can't see the clothes or to disagree with the emperor. The tailor says nothing because he hopes to make money; the emperor's courtiers agree because their jobs depend on him; and the ordinary citizens doubt their own eyes because they believe the emperor is richer and wiser and always right. If the emperor thinks he is wearing a magnificent new suit, no one is going to tell him anything else. So of course the emperor parades through the town in his underwear. Only a child, unaware of how rich and important the emperor is, tells the truth: 'He's not wearing any clothes.'

It can take courage to tell the truth and not be intimidated or influenced by power and money.

SHOOTING THE MESSENGER

Bringing bad news to rich and important people has often been fraught with danger. Sultans and emperors and pharaohs and kings didn't like to hear bad news, and their first command on hearing it was often 'kill him', as if killing the messenger would somehow make the problem go away. No one wanted the job of bad-news messenger. But several cultures came up with a way around this tricky dilemma – the king's courtiers would often offer a condemned prisoner a quick death instead of a grisly one if he delivered the bad news to the king.

THE KING IS DEAD

When no one has the courage to tell rich and important people the truth, it's easy for them to lose touch with reality. It happened to the King of Rock 'n' Roll, Elvis Presley.

Elvis was a phenomenon. Before he was twenty-one, he had made a string of musical hits, and in 1965 he released 'Heartbreak Hotel', 'Hound Dog', 'Don't Be Cruel', 'Blue Suede Shoes' and 'Love Me Tender'. Elvis was declared the King.

No one had ever been so famous. He couldn't appear on the streets without starting a riot. He bought Graceland, a house in Memphis, Tennessee, where he began to spend most of his time surrounded by sycophants (people who just suck up to you) and bodyguards. His private life fell apart. His wife left him. His girlfriends left him. He began to live a very strange life. He turned to prescription drugs – drugs to get up in the morning, drugs to go to bed with at night, drugs before he went on stage and drugs when he came off. The doctors must have known the drugs were dangerous, but no one could say no to the King.

Elvis began his strange eating habits. He loved ice cream, and once ate five chocolate sundaes before breakfast and promptly passed out. He ate mountains of fried food and gained a lot of weight (among his favourite snacks was fried banana and peanut-butter sandwiches!) but no one could say no to Elvis. His musical career went into a decline. He could no longer fit into his stage clothes. He forgot the words to songs and mumbled incoherently. But still no one could tell Elvis the truth.

Even the President of the United States couldn't say no to Elvis. In 1970, Elvis wrote to President Nixon asking to be a 'Federal Agent at Large' to help out in the country's war against drugs. He asked for a police badge; he already had plenty of guns. (Elvis loved guns, and occasionally he'd shoot out TV screens at Graceland if he didn't like the program.) President Nixon met with Elvis and presented him with an honorary agent's badge.

Tragically, in 1977, Elvis was found dead in the toilet at Graceland. There were a total of thirteen drugs in his bloodstream. His body wasn't discovered for five hours after his death. The cause of death was listed as cardiac arrhythmia, but in 1979 Elvis's personal doctor was charged with malpractice and over-prescribing drugs to several patients. He was later acquitted by a jury.

THE FRIED-PEANUT-BUTTER-BANANA-TOASTED SANDWICH

You can make Elvis Presley's favourite food at home!

You need:

bread, preferably white
a banana or two
a jar of peanut-butter (crunchy or smooth)

a frying pan and some butter for frying

Take a slice of bread and spread peanut-butter on one side. Place slices of banana over the peanut-butter and spread more peanut-butter on top. Finish off the sandwich with another slice of white bread.

Sizzle a big dob of butter in a hot frying pan. Butter one side of the sandwich and place it butter-side-down in the pan. Squash the sandwich with an egg-slice until the first side is toasted. Butter the un-toasted side and repeat the process until the sandwich is squashed flat and the peanut-butter is melted.

There you have it!

And a warning – too many of these are not good for your health.

AND NUTHIN' WASHES DOWN A FRIED PEANUT BUTTER SANDWICH LIKE A LONG, COOL GLASS OF COOKING OIL.

THE RISE AND RISE OF THE WEST

WHY DON'T YOU GIVE US YOUR ENTIRE LAND, AND IN RETURN WE'LL GIVE YOU THESE BEADS, MIRRORS, BLANKETS, SMALLPOX, TUBERCULOSIS, PNEUMONIA, INFLUENZA AND WHOOPING COUGH?

TRADE

80,000,000 BCE

If you dropped in to visit Earth eighty million years ago, could you guess which species would dominate the planet in the twentieth century? Probably not. Dinosaurs have been the top species for a couple of hundred million years, and you probably wouldn't even notice the small furry animals scuttling under their feet.

5,000,000 – 100,000 BCE

If you dropped back to visit five million years ago, would you have any better luck? Mammals now dominate the

520 CE
Rise of
mathematics
in India

529 CE
Plato's
Academy
closed

542 CE
Bubonic
plague
ravages
Europe

earth: impressive herds of huge woolly mammoths and ferocious sabre-tooth tigers. A few small bands of ape-like creatures in East Africa don't look very promising in comparison, but if you wait for another 4,900,000 years, a new species will evolve – *homo sapiens*. They're still not very impressive, and they're only one of several hominid (human-like) species vying for living space. Neanderthals have colonised southern Europe and have learned to survive in a very cold climate. They can make sophisticated stone tools. But *homo sapiens* are about to migrate out of Africa...

10,000 BCE

Drop back in to planet Earth twelve thousand years ago and the Neanderthals are extinct, but the small bands of *homo sapiens* have come a long way. There are four million of them now. They've shifted into Europe and across Asia, north to Siberia and south to Australia. They've colonised the American continent and voyaged across the Pacific to settle almost every inhabitable island. They are gathering wild grain and domesticating animals in Turkey and Iran. They've begun to grow crops, build villages and settle down.

622 CE
Beginning
of Islamic
calendar

632 CE
Death of
Mohammed

2000 BCE

Looking down at Earth four thousand years ago, could you guess which culture would dominate the world at the beginning of the twenty-first century? Maize and potatoes are being cultivated in South America. In China people have learned to make chariots, and they can produce bronze and glass. Egypt is being reunified under the Pharaohs. A complex society has emerged on Crete.

500 BCE

How about two and a half thousand years ago? While marble temples and statues are being built in Greece and Socrates is wandering around the marketplace asking questions in ancient Athens, the rest of Europe is still building fortified wooden towns on hilltops.

In China, small states are being unified under the Ch'in dynasty, who began to build the Great Wall of China to stop the 'barbarian' Mongols from invading the country from the north. The Great Wall will eventually stretch to nearly 2500 kilometres long. Constructed of bricks and earth, it will stand eight metres high and will be wide enough to take chariots and horses, with square watchtowers built at regular intervals to keep an eye on the barbarians. China has begun to produce cast iron; they have already been producing silk for centuries.

While Europeans are just learning to navigate the waters of the Mediterranean Sea, the Polynesians have been undertaking a spectacular series of voyages across the Pacific for centuries. Without metal tools or maps, without any way to measure time or instruments to navigate the ocean, they've been sailing across an area of over thirty million square kilometres. Between 1600 and 500 BCE, they have settled Fiji, Samoa and Tonga. A thousand years later, the Polynesians will settle the Islands of Hawaii in the North Pacific, and Easter Island not far from the west coast of South America – one of the most remote and isolated islands on the planet.

Two and a half thousand years ago, the Olmec civilisation had been flourishing on the Gulf Coast of Central America since about 1200 BCE. Even today, we know very little about the Olmecs – we don't even know the name they used for themselves. They didn't develop writing, though they do appear to have originated a complex calender of 365 days. They were an agricultural society and people usually ate maize, fish and dogs. They left huge carved stone heads over two metres high, and, at La Venta in Mexico, a 33-metre-high clay pyramid surrounded by a large plaza and tall basalt columns. We have absolutely no idea what they did there, though it was possibly a ceremonial site. The Olmecs left other monuments carved with scenes of warfare and bloody conquests. Sometime between 400 and 300 BCE, La Venta was violently destroyed and abandoned, bringing an end to the ancient Olmec civilisation. Today, the remains of La Venta have largely been destroyed by modern oil operations, or have been shifted to museums.

1 CE

Would you have any better luck trying to predict the rise of Western culture two thousand years ago? The Roman Empire is at its height. The Han dynasty in China controls an area as far west as central Asia. China has

730 CE
— Printing
in China

a population of sixty million people, and half a million people live in the largest city, Loyang – about the same number as live in ancient Rome. The Chinese invent paper. Some fifteen million people live in the Americas, and the city of Teotihuacan in Mexico has a population of 50,000 people. The Kushan empire is flourishing in north-west Iran, and the Parthian empire controls Mesopotamia and Iran.

1000 CE

Maybe you'd do better a thousand years ago? The Polynesians have settled Aotearoa (New Zealand) in their last great voyage, and every inhabitable island in the Pacific has been colonised. The Vikings reach North America after sailing from Greenland. The Islamic world is the centre of trade and learning, keeping alive the classical Greek tradition of science and mathematics, and extending from Spain to Indonesia and the east coast of Africa. The Chinese are inventing paper money and gunpowder. The Toltec Empire in central Mexico is flourishing. And in western Europe and England? Just a few small squabbling kingdoms.

Getting an Edge

So what happened? How did Western civilisation come to dominate the world? How come we're not all speaking Chinese or Toltec or Latin? How come we're not Neanderthals instead of *homo sapiens*?

For many years, scientists speculated that *homo sapiens* evolved from Neanderthals, or maybe even interbred with them, but recent genetic investigation has

751 CE Paper making spreads to Europe

760 CE Arabs adopt Indian numerals & develop algebra

squashed that idea. There are no *Neanderthal* genes in modern humans. The Neanderthals died out.

Why? They were expert hunters, they made clothes and sophisticated stone tools, they were probably physically stronger than *homo sapiens*, and they had a brain capacity that was slightly larger. A single *Neanderthal* was more than a match for a single *homo sapiens*, and for tens of thousands of years, Neanderthals and *homo sapiens* lived side by side in Europe. But in the end, it would not be the survival of the fittest individual, but survival of the fittest species.

Anthropological studies suggest that *homo sapiens* was a true hunter-gatherer, constantly on the move following wild food and animals, while Neanderthals were more likely to settle down in one area and live off the available resources. *Homo sapiens* were more adaptable to change than Neanderthals. If the herds changed migration routes, *homo sapiens* would follow them. If one source of food dried up, they'd travel until they found another one. Over a long period of time, this adaptability would make a big difference. Recent computer modelling suggests that if Neanderthals were dying at a rate of only two per cent more than *homo sapiens*, they would have become extinct within a thousand years. Adaptability gave *homo sapiens* the edge.

western civilisation

In the year 1000 CE, it would have been almost impossible to predict that Western civilisation (centred in western Europe, England and North America) would dominate world culture by the end of the twentieth century. Similarly today, a few years after 2000 CE, it is

793 CE
Viking
raids
begin

800 CE
First
settlers
reach
Easter
Island

probably impossible to predict which culture will dominate the world in 3000 CE. Over time, little things can make a big difference.

The first stroke of good luck for Western civilisation was geographical and climatic. Much of Europe, Asia and Africa shares a similar climate, and part of a connected landmass. So when crops like wheat and animals such as goats and sheep were domesticated in central Europe and Asia, they quickly spread along routes to the east and west. Similarly, when rice and pigs were domesticated in China, they also spread along the same routes.

Australia, the Americas and southern Africa were not so lucky. By the time crops and animals were being domesticated, the sea levels had risen and Australia and the Americas were isolated. Crops (potato) and animals (lama) were independently domesticated in South America, but they did not spread to North America because they were unable to survive the hot climate of Central America. The situation was much the same in southern Africa – crops and animals from north Africa could not survive the climate in central Africa, and never reached the more favourable climate in the south. Big domesticated mammals such as cattle and buffalo were important to farming communities and early societies. They provided meat, milk, skins, transport and could be used to pull ploughs and war chariots. Some animals could not be domesticated – they were too big or too dangerous – while other animals wouldn't breed in captivity, or were easy to panic or difficult to control. In most of North America, tropical Africa and Australia, there were no large wild animals suitable for domestication, so people living in these areas were less likely to form settled communities, towns and villages.

850 CE
Collapse
of Mayan
culture

EATING TO EXTINCTION

When the Polynesians settled New Zealand about eight hundred years ago, the climate was too cold and wet for the tropical crops and domesticated animals they brought with them. Luckily for the first New Zealanders, there were plenty of native flightless birds that they called 'moa' – 'chicken' in Polynesian. The largest species of moa was more than three metres high and weighed up to 250 kilograms. That's twice as tall as your average person. It wasn't difficult to hunt them: archaeological evidence suggests they were clubbed to death. (You could just hit the big chicken on the head and stick it in the pot.) Unfortunately the evidence can only be archaeological, because by the time white Europeans arrived in the mid-eighteenth century, the moa was virtually extinct.

Even more dramatic events unfolded on Easter Island. Polynesians settled Easter Island more than a thousand years ago. It was (and still is) a small sub-tropical island not particularly suited to agriculture. Only chickens and sweet potatoes survived the long voyage, but when the

Polynesians finally arrived, they found a forest housing a small population of native birds and

animals as well as a variety of trees including an edible palm. The Easter Islanders flourished. They developed picture writing and a sophisticated culture capable of erecting huge carved stone heads. But within 500 years the forests had been completely destroyed. There was no timber left to build houses, so they began to live in caves. There was no wood to build canoes or rafts and go fishing. And, worse, there was almost nothing left to eat. The high culture of the Easter Islanders disintegrated as they fought over the few remaining resources. It's estimated that there were about 2000 people still living on the island when Europeans arrived. Introduced slavery and disease quickly reduced the population to just 111 people by 1877.

THE TRAVELLING IDEA

Along with crops and animals, ideas travelled the trade routes. People learned to make pottery, and then to smelt metal to make tools – both the plough and the sword. These new ideas gave communities an edge. With new farming techniques, there was more than enough food for everyone in the community, so some people became involved in other activities, not just food production. There were priests, warriors, artisans, kings and queens. Soon there was enough leisure time to speed up the development of these activities, producing buildings and artworks of great beauty, developing written languages, complex religious systems, and, of course, making war.

990 CE
Expansion
of Inca
Empire
begins

1000 CE
Vikings
discover
America

Once people had things, there were always other people thinking up new ways to take those things off them. Why raise a crop when you could raid the next village at harvest time and steal theirs? Instead of building a palace, you could raise an army and take someone else's by conquest. Learning how to make war was a profitable business.

Making War

The first organised conflicts were probably raids: a band of warriors from one tribe attacked another tribe to take captives and territory. Once the tribes settled down into villages, loot from the raided village was added to the spoils of war.

At first, warriors would supply their own weapons (clubs and spears), and making war and defending your village was only a part-time job. But as villages became towns and cities, full time warriors (or soldiers) were needed. Sooner or later, someone came up with the bright idea of training the soldiers in fighting skills, and then training the soldiers to fight as a cohesive group, and the first armies came into existence.

With the domestication of the horse six thousand years ago, the nature of warfare changed. On the back of a horse, a warrior could travel greater distances, attack by surprise, and flee swiftly if the need arose. Cavalry

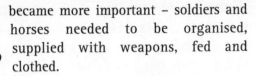

became more important – soldiers and horses needed to be organised, supplied with weapons, fed and clothed.

Three thousand years ago, one of the first military societies emerged in ancient Greece. The city-state of Sparta trained its citizens for war, and Spartans were noted for their military discipline and austerity. They were tough people who exposed newborn babies, leaving them outside for the first days of life so that only the strongest would survive. At the age of seven, boys left their parents and lived in barracks to begin physical training, at twelve they began schooling, and military training at eighteen. Two years later their training was complete, and the Spartan soldier would spend the next ten years of his life living in barracks.

There was one problem with relying on cavalry in Greece: grass, which provided grazing for horses, was in short supply. A change of military tactics was needed, and by 700 BCE the heavily armoured and armed infantry soldier – the 'hoplite' – became the new force of the Greek army. As well as swords, javelins and helmets, each hoplite carried a shield that could be interlocked with the shield carried by the soldier beside him, forming an almost impenetrable barrier. Hoplites were trained to work as a group – the phalanx was a formation usually eight soldiers deep and as many as 200 wide. The phalanx proved capable of defeating both cavalry and less organised soldiers.

ROME MAKES WAR

The ancient Romans refined the art of soldiering and military tactics, and in their heyday Roman armies were unstoppable. At first, only Roman citizens could be soldiers, and each man had to pay for his armour and the upkeep of his family at home. It could be very expensive.

Eventually a Roman general thought up a better way to run the army. He recruited soldiers from out-of-work Romans and promised them a share of all war loot and, if they served for twenty years, a small pension and land. Rome's army had now become professional. Roman soldiers were extremely loyal to their general, whose success or failure would determine their own future.

Julius Caesar's army was a well-disciplined and highly organised force of professional soldiers called legionaries. They wore iron chain-mail armour and helmets, and stout leather sandals capable of standing up to a long march. They carried wooden shields hardened with leather and iron, a throwing spear and a short sword for close combat. A recruit enlisted for twenty-five years, and at full strength each legion consisted of 5000 men.

JULIUS CAESAR

Julius Caesar was a remarkable man. He was noted for being extremely vain, and would comb his hair forward

1100 CE
First
universities
in Europe

1100 CE
Toltecs
build cities
in Mexico

to cover his baldness. He was a notorious ladies' man and had many affairs. But he was also extremely ambitious.

Born to a wealthy, important family, Caesar quickly rose in the political ranks. He was a spellbinding speaker and a forceful writer with an astute grasp of politics, and most of all he was a brilliant military leader. He wrote a long book about his conquest of Gaul, *The Gallic War*, which begins with the famous words:

'The whole of Gaul is divided into three parts...'

No flowery prose or convoluted sentences for Caesar – he gets straight down to business in a clear concise manner, though of course he always manages to present himself and his actions in the best possible light.

His political and military career would see him lead the Roman army to win decisive victories in much of Europe and launch the first expedition against Britain. Eventually his ambition would drive him to march his army on Rome and seize power. He marched his army into Egypt and had an affair with the queen, Cleopatra, before he was off to fight other wars. Caesar wrote to a friend announcing his victories:

'Veni, vidi, vici'

which is a witty word play in Latin, as well as supremely arrogant, meaning, 'I came, I saw, I conquered.'

Things didn't end so well for Julius Caesar. A lot of important people in Rome (including some close friends) began to think Caesar was so ambitious he would destroy the Roman political system entirely. On the Ides of March in 44 BCE, barely a year after he'd returned to Rome from Egypt in triumph, Julius Caesar was attacked in the Senate and stabbed to death by twenty-two senators.

There were twenty-three stab wounds on his body, and several senators were also injured as they accidentally stabbed each other in their frenzied attack. Sixty people were later identified as conspirators in the assassination. After Caesar's death, the Senate proclaimed him to be a god, and built statues and temples in his honour.

IDES?

The early Romans had a complicated system of dividing up the month. *Calends* was the first day of the month (from which our word 'calendar' is derived). *Ides* was the fifteenth day of March, May, July and October, and the thirteenth day of the other months. Originally *Calends* marked the new moon and the *Ides* the full moon; *Nones* were named because they fell nine days before the *Ides*. The days after the Ides were calculated as days before the *Calends* of the next month. Confusing? This system was still used in parts of Europe in the sixteenth century.

Julius Caesar was assassinated on 15 March, and Shakespeare immortalised the words in his play *Julius Caesar* when Caesar is warned, 'Beware the Ides of March!'

The ancient Greeks divided their months into ten-day periods, but Imperial Rome divided the year into seven-day weeks (though the origins of the seven-day week can be traced to the Sumerians and Babylonians). The Romans named the days of the week after the planets: Saturn, the Sun, the Moon, Mars, Mercury, Jupiter and Venus. In Britain, this was later modified and four days of the week were named after Old English and Norse gods and goddesses. Tuesday was named after the god of war, Tiw (Tiw's day), Wednesday after the chief god Odin, or Woden as he became known (Woden's day), Thursday after Thor (Thor's day), the god of thunder and the son of Odin. Similarly the sixth day became Friday (the day of the goddess Frigga – wife of Odin and mother of Thor).

THE JULIAN CALENDAR

Before Julius Caesar, the Romans had based their calendars on two separate systems – the moon and the sun – and to make up the difference between the two, they added an extra month every second year. By the time Caesar came to power, the calendars were out of phase by about three months. The spring equinox came in the winter, and the winter months fell in autumn.

Julius Caesar declared that to fix the problem, one year (46 BCE) should be 445 days. He abolished the lunar calendar and based everything on the sun. He ordered that January, March, May, Quintilis, September and November should have 31 days, and the other months 30 days, except for

February which should have 29 days most years and 30 days in a leap year. In 44 BCE, a grateful Roman Senate voted to rename Quintilis 'July' in honour of the great Caesar.

The Romans fiddled with the system about fifty years later when the Emperor Augustus also had a month named after himself. The month of Sextilis became August, and so that it would have 31 days (obviously Emperors couldn't have short months) they took a day away from February. All this gave them three months of 31 days in succession, so they fiddled a bit more – September and November were reduced to 30 days and October and December raised to 31.

The Julian Calendar was remarkably accurate and would be used for the next sixteen centuries, eventually being imposed on the rest of the world. But there were some minor miscalculations – it was just over eleven minutes too long, which was equivalent to an extra day every 128 years. By 1582, dates were badly out of kilter, and Pope Gregory XIII declared that for that one year, the day after 4 October should be 15 October, and from then on the extra leap year day should be admitted in all years that were multiples of 4, except centenary years that were not also multiples of 400. Many Protestant countries were not so keen on the idea. When Britain adopted the 'new' calendar in 1752, there were riots in the streets when it was announced that eleven days were to be skipped that year. The people demanded the return of the stolen eleven days.

Russia finally adopted the Gregorian system

after the Revolution in 1917. The Greek Orthodox Church still follows the Julian calendar, and Greek Easter and New Year fall at different times each year. The Chinese and Jewish New Year are also celebrated according to their own traditional calendars, but the Gregorian calendar is in use around the world today as the international standard.

SO THE STORY GOES . . . THE ART OF WAR

Before the first Roman legionaries tramped across Europe, China had built the Great Wall and was maintaining a huge standing army along her frontiers. For many centuries before that, small feudal Chinese states had been constantly at war. The Chinese were no strangers to organised warfare.

More than two and a half thousand years ago, a Chinese soldier wrote a profound book on the subject of war and fighting. That book is still in print and studied today – Sun Tzu's *The Art of War*. Its principles were tested on women, or so the story goes...

Sun Tzu was called for an audience with the king of the State of Wu. The king announced that he'd read Sun Tzu's thirteen chapters and wished to test his theory of managing soldiers. 'May the test be applied to women?' the king asked, and when Sun Tzu declared that it could, the king summoned 180 ladies from the palace.

Sun Tzu divided the ladies into two companies and placed one of the king's favourite concubines at the head of each one. Then he told the ladies to each pick up a spear, and asked them if they knew the difference

1215 CE
King John
signs
Magna
Carta

between left and right, front and back. When they replied 'yes', he explained that when he said 'eyes front', they must look straight ahead. When he said 'left turn', they must turn towards their left hand, and towards their right hand when he said 'right turn'. When he said 'about turn', they must face right around towards their back.

The ladies of the court said they understood, but when Sun Tzu ordered the drill to begin, the ladies started giggling and falling about.

Sun Tzu said, 'If the words of command are not clear and distinct, if orders are not thoroughly understood, the general is to blame.'

He started drilling them again until he was sure they understood, but when he gave the command they still fell about laughing.

Sun Tzu said, 'If the words of command are not clear and distinct, if orders are not thoroughly understood, the general is to blame. But if his orders ARE clear, and the soldiers nevertheless disobey, then it is the fault of their officers.'

He ordered the two leaders of the companies to be beheaded. The king was alarmed when he saw the women were about to be executed and he sent a message. 'I am now satisfied as to the general's ability to handle troops. They are two of my favourite concubines. It is my wish they should not be beheaded.'

Sun Tzu replied, 'Having received His Majesty's commission to be the general of his forces, there are certain commands of His Majesty which, acting as his general, I am unable to accept.' He had the concubines beheaded and installed the next two ladies in their place.

Sun Tzu started the drill again, and this time the ladies of the court performed with perfect accuracy and precision.

Sun Tzu sent another message to the king. 'Your soldiers, Sire, are now properly drilled and disciplined, and ready for Your Majesty's inspection. They can be put to any use that their sovereign may desire. Bid them go through fire and water, and they will not disobey.'

The king replied, 'Let the general cease drilling and return to camp. I have no wish to come down and inspect the troops.'

Sun Tzu observed, 'The King is only fond of words, and cannot translate them into deeds.'

When the king realised Sun Tzu knew how to handle an army, he appointed him General. Sun Tzu went on to defeat the Ch'u State to the west and capture the capital, Ying. To the north he put fear into the states of Ch'i and Chin, and his fame spread among the other feudal princes.

Sun Tzu's thirteen chapters of *The Art of War* contain such timeless observations as: 'All warfare is based on deception' and 'There is no instance of a country having benefited from prolonged warfare.'

'In the practical art of war, the best thing of all is to take the enemy's country whole and intact; to shatter and destroy it is not so good. So too, it is better to recapture an army entire than to destroy it, to capture a regiment, a detachment or a company entire than to destroy them ... Hence to fight and conquer in all your battles is not supreme excellence; supreme excellence consists in breaking the enemy's resistance without fighting.'

EUROPE TAKES ON THE REST OF THE WORLD

Europeans became very good at making war; they'd been practising on each other since the Roman Empire fell apart.

About five hundred years ago, greedy European eyes turned to the rest of the world. New technological discoveries allowed them to build ships and navigate the oceans, and voyages of discovery opened up routes to new lands and the lure of gold and wealth. But it wasn't just warfare or guns that would devastate the New World; more deadly were the diseases the Europeans brought with them.

The Spanish conquistador, Hernan Cortez, landed on the coast of Mexico in 1519. Initially Cortez's invasion was successful, and with very little resistance he captured the Aztecs' capital city, Tenochtitlan, and the emperor, Montezuma. Not long after, things started to fall apart. Montezuma was killed and the Aztecs attacked the Spanish invaders. Cortez and his men took heavy losses as they were forced to fight their way back to the coast.

Reinforcements arrived from Spain and six months later Cortez tried again. This time he was successful. When they entered Tenochtitlan, the Spaniards found the houses were filled with dead. They'd died from smallpox. Unlike the Europeans, the native Aztecs had no resistance to the new disease. Smallpox, measles, influenza, typhus, bubonic plague and other infectious diseases continued to ravage the Aztec population, and of an estimated twenty million people when Cortez arrived, a century later there were only about 1.6 million still alive.

Death by Germ

Until the development of the microscope, no one knew that germs spread diseases. When people began to live with domestic animals, they became exposed to new germs, and these germs mutated and happily colonised their new hosts – people. Flu originates with pigs and ducks; measles, tuberculosis and smallpox come from cattle. Once people were crowded together in cities with poor sanitation, germs could really make their move.

The ancient world was not immune. The main rival to Sparta was Athens (home of Socrates, Plato and Aristotle), and in 431 BCE the two city-states went to war. For a while it looked as if Athens' superior maritime power would save the day, but disaster struck in the form of a deadly plague during a siege of the city. Perhaps between one third and a half of the population of Athens died. Ancient writers recorded the progress of the disease, but today we are still not sure what it was. It might have been scarlet fever, or bubonic plague, typhus, smallpox or something completely unknown. The war dragged on for another twenty-seven years, but Athens was ultimately defeated.

But what happened in Athens was nothing compared with the death toll on the native people of the 'newly discovered' lands. Australia was the last great landmass to be discovered by European explorers, and until 1788 when the first English settlement arrived, the Aborigines had been totally isolated. Just as in South America, European diseases such as smallpox, measles, venereal diseases, influenza, whooping cough, pneumonia and tuberculosis devastated the native populations of Australia.

THE ART OF MEDICINE

Before the Greeks evolved the 'scientific approach', disease was thought to be a punishment from the gods.

Though almost all cultures used herbal and folk remedies (the earliest medical textbook was a Chinese book from about 3000 BCE known as the *Great Herbal*), they were no match for serious illness. When you got really sick, praying and offering sacrifices to the gods was all that you could do.

Pythagoras (yes, the Greek mathematician) founded a system of medicine and produced theories of respiration, sight, hearing and brain function. Hippocrates expanded these theories several decades later, and is still regarded by many people as the founder of medical science. The Romans thought the practice of medicine was beneath the dignity of a Roman citizen, and the first physicians were Greek slaves. Julius Caesar improved their social position and granted them the freedom of Rome. But with the fall of Rome and the rise of Christianity, once again people believed sickness was a punishment from God, and the practice of medicine (such as it was) was undertaken by the Church.

In the medieval thirteenth and fourteenth centuries, the Black Death ravaged Europe, killing between one-third and half of the population.

HOW'S IT GOING?

NOT BAD — A LITTLE TOUCH OF THE BLACK DEATH BUT CAN'T COMPLAIN.

1325 CE
Rise of Aztecs in Mexico

Bubonic plague was so terrible, people believed it could only be supernatural in origin, and God must be punishing sinners. A cult of mass flagellation sprang up. Flagellants believed that by whipping themselves and undertaking other physical punishments (such as wearing itchy and uncomfortable 'hair shirts' under thin clothing and spending days on their knees), God might think they'd suffered enough and not punish them with the Black Death. The cult spread all over Europe, and at first the Church thought it was a good idea, but as the flagellants rapidly got out of control, the Pope issued an edict that it was to stop. Those who wouldn't stop were hanged, beheaded or burned. Curiously, the Church sentenced some flagellants to be flogged by priests before the high altar of St Peter's in Rome!

While the Black Death raged, people looked for someone to blame, and anyone who looked or behaved differently immediately fell under suspicion. Rich people, cripples and Jews were easy targets, and persecution quickly followed. In Freiburg and Basel, Jews were herded into large wooden buildings and burned to death. Many Jews fled into eastern Germany and Poland where they were tolerated, and over the centuries large Jewish communities survived into the early twentieth century, although most did not survive the Nazis' 'Final Solution'.

1348 CE
Black Death
ravages
Europe

An Emperor's Ransom

Back in the New World, the Spanish conquistadors were not finished with their brutal conquest of the Americas. A little more than a decade after Cortez, Francisco Pizarro landed in Peru and met the 40,000-strong Inca army of Emperor Atahualpa. Pizarro had only sixty-two soldiers mounted on horses, a dozen muskets and 106 foot soldiers.

It was a massacre. It was always going to be an unequal battle: the Incas were armed only with wooden clubs, stone and bronze hand-axes, and slingshots. Their armour was little more than quilted cloth. They were on foot. They weren't trained to fight as a group, and they took their orders directly from their emperor. In contrast, the Spanish cavalry could move swiftly, armed with steel swords and guns, and protected by steel armour and helmets against the Incas' ineffectual wooden clubs.

The Spanish attacked, firing their muskets and shouting, the cavalry and infantry hurling themselves at the Incas. When their emperor was captured early in the battle, the Incas had no idea what to do. They had never seen horses or guns before, and when the Spanish soldiers began to cut them to pieces with their steel swords, the Incas panicked and fled. The cavalry rode them down, killing and wounding as they pursued the survivors. When the battle was over, seven thousand Incas lay dead, and many more had had their arms cut off or were wounded in other ways. Not a single Spaniard was killed.

Pizarro imprisoned the emperor and demanded an entire room (7 metres long, 5 metres wide and 2.5 metres high) be filled with gold for his ransom. It took eight

1368 CE
Ming
dynasty
in China

months for the Incas to meet Pizarro's demands. He promptly reneged on the deal and executed Atahualpa.

EURoPe GeTS BiG IDeaS

Perhaps more importantly than guns or germs, Pizarro carried the heritage of his culture. The political structure, technology and maritime expertise of Europe allowed Pizarro to sail to South America in search of gold and conquest. Europe was hungry for money and new lands, and was only too happy to finance the expedition, build the ships and equip them with supplies and men, and provide the sailing experience to successfully navigate the journey. While Pizarro himself was illiterate, he had a good idea what to expect in the New World because people such as Christopher Columbus and Cortez had written about their experiences.

News of the Aztec Indians' defeat by the Spanish had not reached the Inca Empire (in fact the two empires didn't know about each other's existence) and the Incas were completely taken by surprise. Worse, the Incas couldn't anticipate that Pizarro was bent on permanent conquest and was not going to leave. When they paid the emperor's ransom in gold, the Incas expected that the Spanish would take the loot and return home. It was not to be.

InDiaNS FiGHt BacK

The North American continent was settled nearly a century after Cortez's adventures in Mexico. Many of the Native American Indian tribes had been quick to adopt the horse and became expert horsemen, in particular the Plains Indians such as the Sioux and Cherokee who mastered both the gun and the horse. They learned from their initial encounters and fought back, inflicting heavy losses and defeats on the white invaders. In 1876, at the battle of Little Bighorn, the Sioux warriors annihilated General Custer's army to the last man.

But it was too late. The invaders were there to stay, and after massive army operations over the next twenty years, the last Native American tribes succumbed to the onslaught.

1500 CE

Let's jump back a few centuries and take a snapshot of the Western world in 1500.

Several decades earlier, the Muslim armies of the Ottoman Empire had captured the city of Constantinople (Istanbul in modern Turkey), the last Christian stronghold in eastern Europe. The rest of Europe was still divided into petty kingdoms, principalities and city-states. New monarchies were beginning to rise in Spain, France and England, but more often than not they were at war with each other, and were not capable of presenting a united front against the Ottoman Empire.

By 1500, the Ottoman Empire had swallowed Greece, Bosnia, Albania and the rest of the Balkans. Within another twenty years, its armies would march towards Budapest and Vienna, raid Italian seaports, and come close to seizing Rome. Indeed, in the sixteenth century, the Islamic world was still the centre of culture, mathematics, engineering, navigation and other technology.

Europe would later 'borrow' much of this culture and learning.

But Islam itself had 'borrowed' from the classical world and China, and Muslim societies had been trading with China for centuries. In fact, it is in China that we find the most advanced, most populated, and most fertile nation in the year 1500.

MinG CHina

The small kingdoms and city-states of China were first unified nearly two thousand years ago when the Great Wall was built. Even so, the Mongol hordes swept over the Wall several times and China was eventually invaded by the armies of Kublai Khan – grandson of Genghis Khan, the great Mongol warlord and emperor.

By the second half of the fourteenth century, the Ming dynasty had emerged to defeat the Mongols and reunite the Chinese empire.

OUR GREAT WALL IS NO MATCH FOR THE VICIOUS MONGOL POLE-VAULTERS.

In 1500, China had an educated civil service running the country based on Confucius's philosophy. China fielded an army of over a million men equipped with factory-produced iron weapons. People and trade goods were transported by boat along an extensive network of man-made canals. They'd invented the magnetic compass and traded with Korea, Japan and South-east Asia. They built huge sea-going junks and explored trade routes to the Pacific islands and eastern Africa, and even brought back giraffes for the entertainment of the emperor.

EMPEROR BANS SAILING

So what went wrong? Why isn't China the dominant culture of the early twenty-first century?

Internal political problems, and new worries about invaders in the north, prompted the emperor to ban the construction of sea-going ships, and reassign the navy to smaller ships on the inland canals. Armies were sent to the north to fortify the Great Wall against the persistent

Mongol hordes. The civil service and bureaucracy became more conservative, and the well-educated elite sneered at the traders and merchants. The emperor forbade overseas trade, and China turned her back on the world.

Within a couple of centuries, the canals were allowed to fall into disrepair, the army was not re-equipped, and the iron factories and other industries were wound down and closed. Printing was restricted to 'approved' scholarly works. There were plagues and floods and war. Just as the first factories were starting up in Europe, the last factories were closing in China. When the Portuguese and Dutch trading ships sailed into Chinese seaports, it was too late – China had closed her doors to the modern world. It would not be until the twentieth century that factories reopened in China.

ISLaM BanS DanGERoUS IDEaS

By the year 1500, the first cracks in the Ottoman Empire were also beginning to show. Eight years previously, the Spanish armies of King Ferdinand had finally defeated and expelled the Muslims from Spain. Ferdinand went on to become the first king of all Spain. He married his cousin Isabella, and together they introduced the Inquisition, expelled the Jews, and financed Columbus's expedition to the Americas. In a few years Pizarro and Cortez would set sail for the New World . . .

Unlike China, the Islamic world was not unified. While the Ottoman Turks were expanding into Europe under Emperor Suleiman the Magnificent, other Muslim states were pushing into India, towards China and West Africa, and would eventually overthrow the Hindu Empire in Java (Indonesia) in the sixteenth century.

At its height, the Ottoman Empire extended further than the Roman Empire; its cities were well-lit, with draining systems, universities, libraries and mosques. But the Ottoman Empire was based on military expansion, and eventually the lines of trade and communication got too long. (Remember Alexander the Great?) Things started to break down. The armies were expensive to maintain and difficult to discipline, and they started helping themselves to local loot. There were internal disputes, and a religious split in the Muslim world when the Shi'ites (based in Iraq and Persia) challenged the accepted Sunni practices and teachings. The printing press was forbidden so people couldn't publish dangerous opinions. There was plague. The army was not re-equipped. The Ottoman empire became preoccupied with its own internal troubles.

Long centuries of seclusion and internal problems meant that neither China nor the Ottoman Empire was able to survive intact the onslaught of European expansion that was soon to follow.

EUROPE OWNS NEARLY EVERYTHING

In the year 1800, Europeans owned or controlled thirty-five per cent of the world's land surface. By 1878 they'd raised that to sixty-seven per cent.

In 1914, Europeans controlled eighty-four per cent of the land surface of the entire planet, and the United Kingdom was still a great power controlling much of the world – it looked as though the sun would never set on the British Empire. The USA had not yet become a world power – it was only fifty years since the end of the American Civil War. The Russian Revolution would not begin for another three years.

By the end of the twentieth century, the Union of Soviet Socialist Republics would collapse in a shambles.

Today, at the beginning of the twenty-first century, Western civilisation dominates the world. But who knows what might happen next? Little things, over time, can make a very big difference.

1510 CE African slaves sent to America

1516 CE Ottomans take Syria, Egypt and Arabia

1519 CE Death of Leonardo da Vinci

1519 CE Cortez begins conquest of Aztecs

1521 CE Suleiman the Magnificent conquers Belgrade

A GRAB BAG OF IDEAS

seeing FURTHER

We take a lot of things for granted about the way we live now – electric lights, telephones, refrigerators, cars – all the amazing technological inventions of the last century or so. We hardly give them a thought every time we make use of them, but imagine trying to live your life without any one of those things.

Remember that we have inherited the learning and cultures of many civilisations. Our achievements would never have been possible without the men and women who went before, and because we stand upon the shoulders of previous generations, we can see a lot further.

Think about this book. The information and ideas contained in it are drawn from every corner of the world and every period in history.

This book is printed on paper. Before paper, people recorded information on stone, which was very difficult to move around, or on heavy clay tablets, or fragile papyrus, or extremely fragile bark. Some cultures invented parchment, made from scraped animal skins, but although parchment had a better surface than paper for writing, it could take the skins from 200 animals to make a single book! So books made of parchment took a long time to make and were very expensive, and they often ran out of supplies.

Paper was first invented by the Chinese in about 105 CE. Bark, grass and rags were soaked for a hundred days before the pulp was mixed with lime and boiled for another eight days. It was washed some more, strained, pounded, bleached and starched. A silk-covered frame was dipped into this gooey mixture, and the thin layer of pulp was left to dry to create a single sheet of paper.

1532 CE
Pizarro begins conquest of Incas

1543 CE
Copernicus publishes theory of celestial bodies

LOOK! I'VE INVENTED 'PAPER'! YOU CAN WRITE ON IT!

IT'LL NEVER TAKE OFF. IT'S TOO FLIMSY! PEOPLE LIKE TO SNUGGLE INTO BED WITH A GOOD, HEAVY STONE TABLET.

Within six hundred years, papermaking reached Korea and Japan, and not long after, paper was being made in India. Islamic troops brought papermaking to Baghdad, where it rapidly replaced parchment, and then carried it on to Egypt where it replaced papyrus. Papermaking travelled across North Africa to Islamic Spain by the tenth century, but the rest of Europe was slow to catch on. It was another four hundred years before France, Germany and Italy began making paper, the English didn't get going until a century later, and the Dutch not for another hundred years after that. The Europeans had no idea that paper had been invented in China a thousand years earlier.

Printing was even more complex. The Chinese first experimented with printing in about 700 CE. At first they used wooden blocks, each of which needed to be carved with lines of text in a very time-consuming process, over and over again as the blocks wore out regularly. They also developed lampblack, an indelible ink suitable for printing, which would eventually find its way to Europe via the Middle East and become known as 'Indian' ink. The Chinese improved their block-printing system and began to carve individual Chinese characters, one for each block, that could be moved about. They had invented

1564 CE
Sea freezes at Marseilles

moveable type. But this was never really going to catch on in a big way because the written Chinese language contained more than 100,000 separate characters! The Mongol Empire picked up printing from the Chinese, and probably spread it west towards Europe. By the end of the thirteenth century, moveable type was being used in Iran.

It was the Koreans who discovered the crucial development of casting metal type at the beginning of the fifteenth century. Now the stage was set for printing to make books affordable for everyone and not just the wealthy elite. It would be a revolutionary idea – nothing would be the same again.

Maybe you bought this book in a bookshop. In the eleventh century, the Chinese government sponsored the printing of the works of Confucius; soon the writings of Lao-Tzu were in print, to be quickly followed by books about medicine, history, geography, philosophy and poetry. There were bookshops in every Chinese city, and China became the first culture where literacy extended beyond a very small group of people.

This book was written in English. The English language is derived from the Germanic, which in turn is derived from the Indo-European language family. English developed in Britain over a period of about 1500 years, beginning with the Anglo-Saxon invaders whose language largely replaced the original Celtic. English was later influenced by Norman French and Latin after the conquest of William the Conqueror in 1066. Modern English contains words from almost every other language in the world, and is still evolving. Written English uses an alphabetic script invented by the Phoenicians three thousand years ago under the influence of other cultures before them.

The numbers used in this book were introduced to the

1607 CE
First permanent English settlement in America

1616 CE
Death of Shakespeare

Europeans by the Arabs, as was the concept of position: the last number written denotes single units (1), the number to its left denotes tens (10), the number to the left of that denotes hundreds (100), and so on. Most importantly, the Arabs also gave us the concept of zero, without which the system doesn't work – 200 would be 2 and 150 would be 15. (So how many loaves of bread are you expected to deliver? Just a few or a truckload?)

The ancient Romans used letters for numbers: I = 1, V = 5, X = 10, L = 50, C = 100, D = 500, and M = 1000. Letters placed to the right were added – thus VI = 6 and VII = 7 – and those to the left were subtracted – IV = 4, IX = 10. To count by tens from 10 to 90, you would write X, XX, XXX, XL, L, LX, LXX, LXXX and XC. So, 1999 becomes MCMXCX and the year 2000 is MM. Try adding up VI and IV. The answer is X. Not too bad? Now try multiplying VI and IV. Subtraction and addition were fairly easy, but, without a zero, multiplication and division were much harder. The answer is XXIV.

In fact, the Arabic numerical system was itself adopted from Indian origins, so today our numbers are known as Hindu-Arabic.

The photographs in this book took just as much innovation. Leonardo da Vinci described the *camera obscura* in 1515 – a darkened chamber where light was admitted through a convex lens and cast a detailed image on a surface to be traced for precise drawings. In 1802, Thomas Wedgwood placed objects on leather that had been treated with silver nitrate (a light-sensitive chemical) and made the first photogram silhouettes. In 1835, Louis Daguerre produced the first camera photograph, and four years later he was offered a pension by the French government and his process was given to the world. In 1844 the first photographic book was published. In 1862 the first aerial photographs were taken over Paris. In 1889, the Eastman company in the USA produced the Kodak camera with the first cheap and easy-to-use roll film. In 1904, the first colour process was patented by the Lumiere brothers. In 1969, photographs were taken on the moon by US astronauts.

Getting Ideas

A few individuals, some known and some forever unknown, have changed the world because of their need to create and understand. We'll never know if some of them were inspired by laziness (I'm sick of walking, I wonder if I can ride that horse?) or by necessity (we have to find something to carry water or we'll die of thirst).

By 6000 BCE, people were making quite sophisticated and beautiful stone axes, knives, chisels and scrapers. These were the end products of a profound technological revolution which allowed people to clear land for farming and to shape wood for a variety of uses, including building. The discovery of metal smelting and shaping would produce stronger and even more effective tools.

Someone first discovered the uses of a lever. It seems obvious to use a strong branch to help shift heavy weights. But if you insert a supporting object (such as a stone or another piece of wood) under the branch at the

INVENTING THE LEVER

right spot, it takes much less effort to lift a heavy rock. This 'right spot' is the fulcrum, and it effectively divides the branch into two arms, a short one under the rock and a long one you push down on.

The lever is a powerful tool. The ancient Greek mathematician Archimedes declared:

> 'Give me a place to stand, and with a lever I will move the earth.'

Archimedes understood the principle of the lever. We still use levers today – crowbars, wheelbarrows, nutcrackers and tongs (to name just a few).

Back to the wheel

The wheel was probably early man's greatest invention, and while many civilisations invented the wheel, it was not always used for transport. Wheeled transport needs a couple of other factors to be really effective – first it needs a suitable terrain, or good roads. It takes a lot of effort to cut roads through mountains and steep slopes; in tropical areas, roads get washed away in the monsoon season; and in desert areas, roads are continually covered up with drifting sand.

In ancient Egypt, the Nile River provided an easy form of transport – boats – and wheeled vehicles were first developed for making war. Heavy or bulky items such as stone for building, or the grain harvest, were shifted by boat.

LOOK! I'VE INVENTED THE CHEESE PLATTER!

For wheeled transport to be really effective, you also needed a suitable domestic animal to pull the load. Although the Aztecs and the Incas occasionally made wheeled toys, they were never developed for transport – either the terrain was too steep or there were convenient waterways for boats. There were also no suitable large domestic animals in the Americas, though they did use the llama as a pack animal.

WILD IDEAS

Sometimes new discoveries don't just change history, they also cause us to change the way we *see* history.

When Democritus came up with his theory of atoms nearly two and a half thousand years ago, it was no more than that – a theory. There were hundreds of other theories around at the time. It was not until modern scientific discoveries confirmed that Democritus was on the right track that he became so important. Who knows? Maybe other philosophers' wild ideas and theories might also prove to be right.

During the second half of the seventeenth century, a German mathematician and philosopher came up with a theory that everything consisted of minute elements he called 'monads'. Leibniz believed they were not so much particles as metaphysical forces, whose individual properties determined their past, present and future. Sound crazy? Remember, Leibniz was also a mathematician who worked out differential and integral calculus. Maybe one day he will be proved to have been on the right track all along.

SO THE STORY GOES . . .
NAKED MAN RUNS THROUGH STREETS

Archimedes was the man who noticed that the water level rose and fell as he got into and out of the bath. He was so excited by his idea that he jumped from the bath and ran through the streets shouting 'Eureka!' – Greek for 'I've found it!' He'd discovered the principle of fluid displacement.

DISCOVERING DIMENSIONS

Another Greek mathematician, Euclid, developed a simple way to describe the world in three dimensions. It's called Euclidean geometry, and we still use it today:

A point has no dimensions.
A line has one dimension – length.
A plane has two dimensions – length and width.
A solid has three dimensions – length, width and
    height.

POINTLESS
DRAWING.

We live in a three-dimensional world. It was not until the twentieth century that Albert Einstein would add a fourth dimension – time. When Albert Einstein came up with his most famous equation, $E = mc^2$, he would change the world forever. His theories would release atomic power and the atom bomb; they would lead to scientists developing the 'big bang' theory of creation.

PURE GENIUS

Without a doubt, Albert Einstein was a genius – a person with extraordinary powers of intellect, imagination or invention.

How do you measure genius? And where do geniuses come from? The second question is the easiest – we don't know. Perfectly ordinary families produce geniuses. While talents such as a gift for music or mathematics often run in families, true genius does not.

During the twentieth century, psychologists became interested in measuring intelligence. They developed tests to measure memory, reasoning ability and comprehension. Finally the IQ (Intelligence Quotient) test was developed. A 'normal' IQ ranges from 85 to 115. It's estimated that only one per cent of people have IQs over 135. Geniuses have IQs above 145. IQ scores of 200+ are 'universal geniuses', and there are so few of them that scores over 200 are considered unmeasurable.

Of course, IQ tests don't measure success or happiness, and it has been argued that they measure nothing more than your ability to do IQ tests. But they can be a bit of fun for measuring genius.

Psychologists have studied historical geniuses and made educated guesses of their IQs. The German writer Johann Goethe tops the list with a score of 210. The Italian Renaissance artist Leonardo da Vinci and the German philosopher Leibniz both come in at 205. Further down the list is Galileo, the Italian astronomer, at 185. Charles Darwin, the naturalist, and the Austrian composer Mozart both score 165. The Dutch painter Rembrandt sits at 155, and the French writer George Sand at 150. It's even been suggested that Einstein (considered the universal genius of the twentieth century) may have had an IQ of only 160!

HYPatia

So far there's been only one woman recorded on the 'universal genius' list, a Greek mathematician and philosopher of renowned beauty and intellect. Her brutal murder would coincide with education for women entering the dark ages for the next 1500 years.

Hypatia was born in about 350 CE. Her father was a very educated man, a scholar and teacher of mathematics in Alexandria, in Egypt. He educated his daughter, and she in turn helped him write several books on mathematics. She went on to become the head of a school at Alexandria and lectured on mathematics and philosophy. She wrote many books, none of which have survived, and we only know about them because other ancient writers referred to them.

It was a bad time to be an educated woman in Alexandria. The early Christians believed philosophy and science to be pagan activities that should be stamped out. Hypatia became the focal point of bloody riots between the Christians and non-Christians. She was returning home one night when her carriage was set upon by a Christian mob. She was dragged from the carriage, stripped naked and beaten to death with stones. Her eyes were ripped out before she died, her body was torn limb from limb, and her mangled remains were thrown on a fire at the Library of Alexandria.

BURNING THE BOOKS

The great library at Alexandria was founded in the third century BCE by one of the Greek Egyptian kings on the advice of his literary adviser. Phalereus suggested that the king should collect copies of all the known books in the world and set up a universal library. In those days, a book was generally a long papyrus roll glued at the ends to wooden rods so that it could be gradually unrolled and read. Books were written by hand and copied by scribes; they were precious and fragile objects. Some rolls were as much as 50 metres long, but gradually they came to be 5 to 6 metres long. Long written works would be divided into sections (also called 'books') that fitted onto a standard length of papyrus.

The king's buyers scoured the known world for books. Travellers to Egypt had to hand over any books they might have. A copy was made and returned to the owner, while the originals were placed in the library. At its peak, the Library of Alexandria may have held more than half a million books, and it took several buildings to hold the collection. The library made Alexandria the intellectual capital of the world. Archimedes and Euclid both lived and worked in Alexandria.

A series of fires and thefts during the Roman period gradually destroyed the library. At Queen Cleopatra's urging, Julius Caesar helped himself to thousands of books and intended to ship them back to Rome. Unfortunately, Caesar found himself in a bit of trouble before he left Alexandria, and during the fighting the buildings near the harbour were set alight, destroying perhaps as many as 40,000 books. There was further destruction of the library when the Alexandrian people twice revolted against Rome in the third century. The early Christians destroyed more books in the next century. Finally in the seventh century the Muslim Arabs took control of the library and most of what remained was destroyed.

1752 CE
Britain
adopts
Gregorian
calendar

So the story goes... When the Arab general asked his superiors what he should do with the infidels' books, he was told that unless they agreed with the Koran they should be destroyed. But others have squarely blamed the destruction of the last of the library's collection on the Christians. We shall never know, nor shall we know exactly how many books were destroyed and lost forever.

What we do know is that with the rise of Christianity and Islam, the custom of burning an enemy's books rose to new heights. Maybe they wanted to show their disdain for their victims, or maybe they just enjoyed a good bonfire. In 373 CE, the Christian Roman emperor Valens ordered all non-Christian books to be burnt. In 637 CE, the Muslim Arabs conquered Iran and destroyed the books of the Zoroastrian Persians. The Crusaders burned Muslim books when they captured Tripoli in 1109 and Constantinople in 1204, as did the Spaniards when they threw out the Moors. During the Spanish conquest of the New World, the entire writings of the Incas and Aztecs were burned as 'superstition and lies of the devil'.

1760 CE
Age of
Enlightenment

A Universal Genius For All Time

Although Goethe outranks Leonardo da Vinci on the estimated IQ score, it is Leonardo who is generally considered to be the greatest all-round genius who ever lived.

Today we remember Leonardo as the sublime artist who painted *The Last Supper* on a wall of a convent in Milan, and who captured the *Mona Lisa*'s enigmatic smile. But when Leonardo da Vinci wrote to the ruling family in Milan and asked for a job, he stressed his achievements as a military engineer. His ability as an artist came well down the list.

Leonardo was the illegitimate son of an Italian public official and a peasant girl. His father took him into his home when he was just a baby, and his mother married someone else and shifted to another town. As a boy, Leonardo had access to books and drawing and painting materials in the house. When he was fifteen, his father apprenticed him to a famous artist, Verrocchio. So the story goes ... When young Leonardo painted an angel in one of his master's paintings, Verrocchio declared it was so much better than his own work that he vowed never to paint again.

Leonardo soon gained work as an independent artist and did get the job in Milan, where he not only painted and sculpted but also designed weapons, buildings and machinery. He produced work on nature, flying machines, geometry, mechanics, canals and architecture. He studied everything and made his own observations, dissecting corpses to study anatomy and ponder on universal truths.

1775 CE
American
Revolution

1778 CE
Death
of
Voltaire

He recorded his studies in meticulously illustrated notebooks. Leonardo da Vinci was left-handed, and he developed a system of writing backwards which can only be deciphered easily with a mirror.

In 1516, when Leonardo was an old man, the King of France offered him a position as Premier Painter, Engineer and Architect to the King. It was a cushy job with an allowance and a large house near the royal chateau. Leonardo died on 2 May 1519, in France, and legend says the king cradled Leonardo's head in his arms while he died.

CHARLES DARWIN

Charles Darwin wrote one of the most controversial books ever written. When *The Origin of Species* was first published, it sparked a huge religious outcry, and had an enormous impact on how people thought about 'the human race'. But Darwin was only trying to explain what he had observed.

When Charles Darwin was twenty-one years old, he got a job as a naturalist on a British science expedition sailing around the world. In South America, he found fossils of extinct species that were similar to modern ones. In the Galapagos Islands in the Pacific, he noticed species of animals and plants that were different but similar to species in South America. He continued studying plants and animals, collecting specimens and taking notes for further study back in England.

Over the next two decades, Darwin formulated his theory of evolutionary selection, and finally – twenty-three years after he returned from his inspirational voyage – he published *The Origin of Species*. He argued that random variations occur within any species, and that an organism's ability to survive (or not) is determined by its ability to adapt to its environment. Thus different species can develop or 'evolve' in different areas, over millions of years, from the same ancestral species.

Darwin was a reserved scholarly man, but his theories caused a furore. The Christian Church taught that God had created the world in seven days, and had made man in his own image. Several eminent people had calculated exactly how old the world was according to biblical tradition, so how could a species take millions of years to form? And surely Darwin was not suggesting that humans had evolved from the same species as apes? People were not descended from monkeys!

Eventually Darwin's ideas caught on, and his theories of evolution have had a lasting effect on how we see ourselves today.

THE MONKEY TRIAL

Darwin's theories are still controversial in many places.

In 1925, a Tennessee high-school science teacher, John Scopes, was arrested and charged with 'teaching evolutionary theories that denied the story of creation in the Bible'. It was to be a test case for a new Tennessee law that forbade teaching any theory that man had evolved from a lower form of life. At the time, Christian fundamentalists were a strong political force in Tennessee, and they believed in the literal truth of the Bible. They felt that teaching Darwin's scientific theory would undermine students' Christian beliefs.

It was a very famous trial in a crowded courtroom over eleven long hot days. The jury deliberated for nine minutes before they brought in a verdict of guilty. John Scopes was convicted. The conviction was overturned a year later on a technicality, but the law against teaching evolution remained on the books until 1967 – though by then, Darwin's evolutionary theories were taught in most high schools.

John Scopes left teaching and pursued further studies in science.

A Lot of sweat

The American scientist and inventor Thomas Edison once said:

'Genius is one per cent inspiration and ninety-nine per cent perspiration.'

1807 CE
Slave
trade
abolished
in British
Empire

Edison was born in 1847, and after only three months of school, his teacher thought he was such a strange child that his mother decided to teach him at home. He was a voracious reader, with a particular love of chemistry and electricity. At the time, electricity was considered a novelty – there were no electrical appliances and no one was quite sure what electricity could be used for. Thomas Edison would change all that.

By the time Edison was twelve, he had a job selling newspapers, and spent his free time reading at the library. He saved his money, bought a second-hand printing press and began publishing his own newspaper. After he rescued a child from the path of a train, the child's father was so grateful he offered to teach the young Edison telegraphy (Morse code), which was in such high demand that Edison quickly got a job. In 1868, Edison patented his first invention – an electric vote-recording machine – but when he demonstrated it he was told it was not practical. Edison vowed he would never again invent anything without first being sure it was needed.

In 1871, while Edison was waiting for a job interview, a telegraph broke down and he fixed it while he was waiting. The company offered him a better job, and Edison went on to invent an improved 'ticker' machine for reporting stock prices. He offered the machine for sale, but he wasn't game to ask for the money he wanted – $5000. He let the buyers suggest a price and they paid him $40,000! With the money, Edison set up an 'invention factory' where he and his assistants turned out a steady stream of inventions – a new patent every five days. In his lifetime, Edison patented 1093 inventions.

Edison's most famous invention was the light bulb, but he also developed the phonograph for recording

1818 CE
Britain
rules
India

sound, and the kinetoscope for viewing moving film. He improved Alexander Graham Bell's invention, the telephone. By the time Edison died, electricity was no longer a novelty, and entire cities were lit by electric light.

EVERYDAY INVENTIONS

We take for granted so many things that make our lives easier – we use them every day and don't give them a second thought. Yet none of these everyday inventions would be around today if someone hadn't come up with the bright idea in the first place.

The vacuum cleaner was invented in 1902 by British inventor Cecil Booth. He devised a huge commercial vacuum cleaner that was so large it was mounted on a wagon in the street, and long hoses were passed through the window. Fashionable London ladies held vacuum-cleaning parties so they could watch the machine work. The first portable vacuum cleaners went on sale in America in 1905, and weighed 42 kilograms.

A French man who was determined to invent a protective transparent covering for tablecloths invented cellophane in 1912. It took him eight years, and while cellophane was never used to keep tablecloths clean, it did revolutionise packaging.

The electric blanket was invented in 1926. An American physician had invented heating pads for patients several years earlier, but it was not until after the First World War, when a British welfare agency began looking around for something ex-soldiers could do, that 'Thermega underblankets' were produced commercially.

1829 CE
Suttee made illegal in India

Sticky tape – cellulose self-adhesive tape – went on sale in 1928. It was invented by the 3M company. In 1979, the same company would invent post-it notes which 'stick without sticking'. The special adhesive used in post-it notes had been invented a few years earlier, but no one had been able to think of any suitable use. One employee had tried using the glue to make bookmarks, and one day he wrote a note on a bookmark, stuck it on a report and sent it to his boss. His boss wrote his reply on the note and sent it back – and Arthur Fry suddenly realised what the 'stick without sticking' glue could be used for.

Typing correction fluid was invented by the mother of a boy who would go on to become a member of a famous pop group in the 1960s – The Monkees. Bette Nesmith was a typist – not a very good typist – and she was looking for a way to fix all her mistakes. She invented correction fluid on her kitchen table. With the help of her son, Michael, she began to produce it in the garage. She sold her business in 1979 for $47 million, and her typing correction fluid became Liquid Paper.

FORGOTTEN INVENTIONS
The Pop-Up Kettle.

YAARGH!

SCIENTIST GETS EGG ON FACE

The microwave oven was invented in 1945. A scientist working for a company in Massachusetts was standing in front of a radar power tube one day, and when he reached into his pocket for a snack, he discovered that his candy bar was a gooey melted mess. He decided to run an experiment. He placed an egg in a kettle with a hole cut in one side and placed it in front of the radar power tube. One of his colleagues lifted the lid to see what was happening, and was instantly covered in gooey egg as the shell exploded under pressure. The first microwave went on sale in 1947 and cost $3000.

AUSSIES Invent DUAL-FLUSH Toilet

Australia is considered to be the driest continent on Earth, so perhaps it's not surprising that dual-flush toilets were invented in Australia. Developed in the 1980s, they are estimated to save 32,000 litres of water per year in the average household, offering the choice between full-flush (six litres) and half-flush (three litres). Dual-flush toilets are now compulsory in most Australian states, and are exported to more than thirty countries worldwide.

Australia's fast-growing wine industry was responsible for the invention of the wine cask. Once a bottle of wine is opened to the air, the wine goes 'off' in a couple of days. The plastic bag inside wine casks collapses as wine is poured out, and keeps the air away from the remaining wine, allowing it to be kept for a lot longer without going off.

Australia was also the first country to use plastic banknotes, which last ten times longer than paper notes. Plastic money is much harder to counterfeit than paper money, and so plastic banknotes were the world's first long-lasting, counterfeit-resistant money in circulation. Today, Australia manufactures plastic money for a number of other countries around the world.

AUSSIE INVENTS ORANGE BLACK BOX

In 1953, an Australian chemist was sent as part of a team to investigate air crashes. Dave Warren thought he could have learned a lot about the crashes by talking to the pilots, but unfortunately the pilots were dead. Dave came up with the idea of building a machine that could survive a crash, and which would record what happened in the cockpit and flight instruments. No one in Australia was interested, and he had to take his idea overseas, where they thought it was a great idea, and Black Box recorders were manufactured in the UK and USA. Today, every commercial plane carries a Black Box recorder, though they are now coloured orange to make them easier to find after a crash. Unfortunately, Dave Warren never made any money out of his invention.

AUSSIE HELPS INVENT MOULD

At Oxford University in 1939, an Australian medical researcher named Howard Florey and a German biochemist named Ernst Chain began working on an interesting mould. The mould had first been noticed growing on a discarded culture dish by an English scientist several years earlier. It was a very interesting mould that appeared to stop bacteria from growing anywhere near it. Florey and Chain's research demonstrated that the mould could fight bacterial infection in humans. It was penicillin, and it would save untold millions of lives around the world.

A Lost Genius

Geniuses don't always go on to fulfil their potential, and a high IQ isn't a guarantee of a happy and successful life.

William James Sidis was born on April Fools' Day in 1891 to Russian immigrant parents in America. His parents were both brilliant; his father was an academic at Harvard, and his mother temporarily gave up her medical career to devote herself to creating intellectual greatness in their new son.

Young William went on to exceed their wildest expectations. He was talking before he was one year old, and he could spell a few weeks later. He started reading the *New York Times* when he was eighteen months old. He started typing at three and wrote four books between the ages of four and eight. He learned to read Greek when he was four. At six he learned Russian, French, German and Hebrew, followed by Turkish and Armenian – he could learn a whole language in one day. He had total recall of everything he read.

William started school at age six and finished primary school in six months. He passed the entry exam for Harvard Medical School at seven and the Massachusetts Insitute of Technology entrance exam at eight. He attempted to enrol at Harvard at nine, but had to wait until he was eleven – the youngest student ever to enrol. At age eleven, he lectured on mathematics at Harvard. He graduated when he was sixteen, and was offered a job as a professor of mathematics at another university, but the students gave him such a hard time that he quit and entered Harvard Law School.

WILLIAM SIDIS

...AND IF WE CALCULATE THE SUBSET OF THE MEAN DERIVATIVE OF THE TWO INTEGERS... OH BOTHER! I'VE POOPED MY NAPPY.

$$\frac{x}{y} = \frac{x^3}{xy}$$

$$x = \frac{24x}{3}$$

But all was not well with William Sidis.

Over the next few years, he became interested in politics, becoming a socialist and ending up in jail in 1918 during a communist anti-war rally. The newspapers hounded him. They made his life a misery and he retreated to his own strange world. He continued to write books, some under his own name and others under pseudonyms, but many he just forgot about or lost. He became totally immersed in his hobby – collecting streetcar transfers (tram tickets), and published a book about them. He wrote

1870 CE
Death
of
Charles
Dickens

1878 CE
British
Factory
Acts
passed

a complete guide to public transport in Columbia and the north-eastern suburbs of Boston, and knew the details of most routes in the USA.

Sidis vowed never to marry and remained celibate his whole life, but when he died from a brain haemorrhage in 1944, he was still carrying a photograph of a woman he'd met in jail many years previously. She was Martha Foley, an Irish socialist who long ago had married someone else. All his life, Sidis had disregarded art and music, any sort of physical activity, anything to do with money, and also, it would appear, love and companionship.

The world will never know what we lost when William Sidis turned his back on society and dropped out. His IQ has been assessed as somewhere between 250 and 300, and he was arguably the brightest human who ever existed.

SO THE STORY GOES . . .
IT SEEMED LIKE A GOOD IDEA AT THE TIME

Some people have a natural genius for getting it wrong. Every year, the Darwin Awards recognise the person who has done the human gene pool the greatest service by eliminating themselves by their own stupidity. Previous winners have included the man who was killed by a soft-drink machine that toppled over and crushed him while he was trying to extract a free drink. Honourable mentions have gone to the salesman who was reading a sales manual when his car smashed into a pole in the median strip of a highway, the man who stole a hot dog and then choked to death on it when he shoved it in his mouth as he walked out the door, and the thieves who

1880 CE
Ned Kelly
hung

1884 CE
Mignonette
sinks

attempted to steal copper wire off live electrical lines and electrocuted themselves.

Some of these stories have become urban legends – cautionary tales and modern fables – they happened to a friend of a friend, and even if they're not true, they should be.

There's the one about the office show-off in New York who used to hurl himself at the glass windows in his fiftieth-floor office, laughing at his visitors' horrified reactions as he bounced off the toughened glass . . . until the day when he'd done it once too often, and it was not the glass that gave way but the window fixings, and he plummeted fifty stories to the pavement below.

It must have seemed like a good idea at the time . . . Larry Walters of Los Angeles always wanted to fly. He joined the airforce but his poor eyesight disqualified him from becoming a pilot. He left the service and became a truck driver, watching the jet fighters fly over his backyard. As he sat in his chair, he still dreamed about flying. One day, Larry had an idea. He purchased forty-five weather balloons from the surplus store and several tanks of helium gas. Larry attached the weather balloons to his plastic garden chair, tethered the chair to his jeep, and inflated the balloons. Then he went inside and collected his supplies: a few sandwiches, cans of beer, and an air-rifle so he could shoot out the balloons when he wanted to come back down. Everything was set. Larry sat in his chair and cut the cord to his jeep. It was a major miscalculation. Larry's garden chair did not slowly ascend, but shot up until he levelled out at about 5000 metres. It was too high to shoot out the balloons

1893 CE
Women
given the
vote in
New
Zealand

without risking toppling the chair and tipping himself out. It was very cold up there, and it was a long, long way down. Larry Walters was alone, frightened, helplessly drifting across the suburbs of Los Angeles. He drifted towards the flight path of the Los Angeles International Airport, where startled pilots reported they had passed a man in a garden chair with a gun at about 5000 feet. One of them radioed the Federal Aviation Administration. Rescue helicopters were dispatched to investigate. Eventually, Larry popped a few balloons with his air-rifle and began to descend, until the balloons became entangled in power lines and blacked out the area. Larry Walters was arrested and fined $1500 by the FAA.

Maybe Paul Queroli dreamed of being a pilot, but we'll never really know what prompted his experiment with speed. Perhaps it just seemed like a good idea at the time. The Arizona Highway Patrol was called to investigate a smouldering pile of metal embedded 38 metres up the side of a cliff. There was very little to see, but it didn't look like an aeroplane, it looked like a car. The investigators finally worked out what had happened. Somehow Paul Queroli had acquired a solid-fuel rocket that was normally used to assist heavy military planes take off from short runways. He'd driven his Chevrolet Impala car out to the desert to a long straight stretch of road, attached the rocket, and jumped in. Approximately five kilometres from the crash site, the investigators discovered scorched and melted asphalt, and that's where they concluded Paul had turned on the rocket. They calculated it would have taken five seconds for the

Chevy to reach a speed in excess of 590 kilometres per hour, and the car would have remained at that speed for an extra twenty to twenty-five seconds. The car stayed on the road for about 4.2 kilometres before the driver applied the brakes. The brakes melted, the tyres blew out and left thick rubber marks on the road surface, and then the car became airborne for another 2.4 kilometres. It impacted the cliff at a height of 38 metres. Paul Queroli was identified from small fragments of bone and teeth extracted from the wreckage.

For many years, this story (or variations of it) was considered to be true, but in fact the Arizona Highway Patrol has confirmed that it never happened. Paul Queroli and his homemade jet-propelled car are the stuff of urban legends – a cautionary tale of the deadly mixture of technology and human stupidity.

THE ART OF BEING WRONG

Geniuses and inventors don't just have to be smart – they also have to have the courage to say or try something completely new, and to stand by their convictions when other people are shouting them down. People we regard as visionaries today were often regarded as mad crackpots in their own time. But history sometimes proves they were right all along. For others, history proves they were dead wrong.

'Heaven and earth were created all together in the same instant, on October 23rd, 4004 BC at nine o'clock

1902 CE
Women given
the vote in
Australia

1905 CE
Einstein
publishes
theory of
relativity

1911 CE
Chinese
Revolution

1912 CE
Titanic
sinks

in the morning.' (Sir John Lightfoot, Vice-Chancellor of Cambridge University, just before the publication of Charles Darwin's *Origin of Species* in 1859)

'Flight by machines heavier than air is unpractical and insignificant, if not utterly impossible.' (Simon Newcomb, *US Astronomer*, 1903)

'The actual building of roads devoted to motor cars is not for the near future, in spite of many rumours to that effect.' (*Harper's Weekly*, 1902)

'You will never amount to very much.' (A Munich schoolmaster to Albert Einstein, aged 10)

'I can accept the theory of relativity as little as I can accept the existence of atoms and other such dogma.' (Ernst Mach, Professor of Physics, University of Vienna)

'This is the biggest fool thing we have ever done ... The atomic bomb will never go off, and I speak as an expert in explosives.' (Admiral William Leahy, 1945)

'Television won't be able to hold onto any market it captures after the first six months. People will soon get tired of staring at a plywood box every night.' (Darryl F. Zanuck, movie producer)

'It can be taken for granted that before 1980 ships, aircraft, locomotives, and even automobiles will be atomically fuelled.' (David Sarnoff, US radio executive, 1956)

'We don't like their sound. Groups of guitars are on the way out.' (Decca Recording Company when they turned down the Beatles in 1962)

'I think there is a world market for maybe five computers.' (Thomas Watson, chairman of IBM, 1943)

THE LAST SOLDIER

Some people don't fit easily into categories – genius or dummy, hero or villain, sane or mad – yet their stories are still extraordinary examples of the human spirit.

Lieutenant Hiro Onoda received his last orders in the final months of World War II: 'No Surrender!' It was the code of the Japanese samurai, and Lieutenant Onoda followed it for the next thirty years.

Onoda had been sent by the Japanese Army to a small island in the Philippines to lead attacks against enemy airfields. On 28 February 1945, American troops attacked the island, and in a four-day battle destroyed almost all Japanese resistance, except for a few small bands of survivors like the one led by Lieutenant Onoda. The survivors melted into the jungle and continued to fight, unaware that Japanese forces surrendered a few months later on 14 August.

During the next year, most of the Japanese soldiers gave themselves up, only to be told that World War II was over. But Onoda and his three comrades continued to resist. Over the next few years, leaflets were distributed all over the island explaining that the war had ended. Planes dropped letters and photographs from the three men's families back home, begging them to surrender. Onoda and his companions were convinced it was just a trick. They fought on.

The men were constantly on the move, sleeping in the open except for the wet season when they lived in makeshift huts. They learned to mend their clothes with fibres collected from the jungle. They used palm leaves as toilet paper. Food was one of their main problems, and they largely lived on bananas and coconuts, but they would occasionally kill a local cow, or 'requisition' supplies from the villagers at gunpoint during daring night raids. The villagers named the soldiers 'the mountain devils'.

One of the men was killed in 1953 when he stood up and aimed his rifle at a search party sent to find them. There were many search parties over the next two decades. Onoda's brother and sister, and then another brother, travelled to the island, using microphones to plead with Onoda to surrender. He was still convinced it was just a trick, and when Onoda's last companion was killed in 1972 during one of their night raids, Lieutenant Onoda was totally alone.

In 1974, a young Japanese student dropped out of university and vowed he would find Onoda and convince him to surrender. He travelled to the island, and after only four days of searching, he found Onoda – the lieutenant was about to shoot him when the young man spoke to him in Japanese. He explained to Onoda that the war was over and it was time for him to return to Japan. Still

1933 CE
Hitler rises
to power in
Germany

1935 CE
Stalin
purges
communist
party

1939–
1945 CE
World War II

Onoda was not convinced, and he vowed he would only surrender if his superior officer told him to.

In March 1974, Major Taniguchi, who was by then employed in a bookshop, travelled to the island for a secret meeting with Lieutenant Onoda. Under the cover of darkness, Onoda approached the camp, recognised his old superior officer, snapped to attention and saluted. 'Lieutenant Onoda, sir, reporting for orders.'

'Good for you.' Taniguchi patted him on the back and then proceeded to order him to cease all military activities and operations. Slowly Onoda unloaded his rifle and surrendered his weapon. His war was over. Much to the disgust of the local villagers, Onoda was pardoned for all the crimes he'd committed over the last thirty years. He returned to Japan to a hero's welcome. He had done his duty with true samurai spirit.

But Onoda never really adjusted to modern life in Japan. He wrote his memoirs and used the money to buy a ranch in Brazil. He began lecturing schoolchildren about nature and health.

Why did Lieutenant Onoda persist with his single-man war for so many years? Was it misplaced loyalty, or military training and cultural expectation? Stubbornness? Or just a complete lack of common sense? Was he a truly individual spirit with incredible moral courage, or was he so brainwashed by his military training that he couldn't think for himself at all?

1946 CE
First electronic computer built

1946–1949 CE
Civil war in China

1947 CE
India becomes independent

1947 CE
Cold War

1948 CE
Apartheid laws passed in South Africa

1948 CE
Mohandas Gandhi assassinated

1950 CE
Senator McCarthy denounces communists

A FINAL WORD

One of the most exciting and frustrating aspects of history is learning how things are interlinked. Remember Crassus, the richest man in Rome? He pops up again as the Roman general who crushed the slave rebellion led by Spartacus and ordered all the survivors to be crucified along the road leading back to Rome. Crassus also lent a lot of money to Julius Caesar who was deeply in his debt, and he later formed a triumvirate (a group of three men in authority) with Caesar and another general, Pompey, in a bid to seize power in Rome.

Crassus came to a sticky end. He fancied himself as a great general; he'd defeated Spartacus, hadn't he? But Crassus overestimated his own ability, and when he invaded Mesopotamia, his army was defeated, he was captured and put to death, and his severed head was sent back to Rome.

Not only are people interlinked, but events and subjects as well. Reading about Julius Caesar leads to calendars and time and geography and military strategy and technological developments, which leads to art and science and astronomy and biology and psychology. It just goes on and on until you feel like Socrates: the more you learn the less you realise you know.

1953 CE
Death of
Stalin

1961 CE
Structure
of DNA
discovered

What can we learn from history? Is there any point to all those endless dates and names and places? There's an old maxim that says 'those who do not learn from history are condemned to repeat its mistakes'. Civilisations that are isolated, or suppress learning, eventually begin to stagnate and fall into decline. Cultures that remain receptive to debate and new ideas have the capacity to adapt and survive. Communities who fail to defend the rights and freedoms of all their citizens risk heading towards tyranny. People who stop treating each other with respect and tolerance are on the road to prejudice and, ultimately, genocide.

We can learn how not to do it from the experiences of China and the Ottoman Empire, the almost-extinction of the Easter Islanders, the rise of fascism and the Nazis, the excesses of Stalin's regime, and the persecution of minority groups in America. We can also learn the positive lessons of history from Socrates and the flowering of ancient Greek culture, from the Renaissance and the explosion of new ideas, from Voltaire and the great thinkers of the Age of Enlightenment, from the extraordinary bravery of the Danish people during World War II, and from the non-violent protests of Mahatma Gandhi and Dr Martin Luther King. Each and every one of us has the capacity to ask the big questions and answer them for ourselves.

Think carefully, because the future is in your hands.

1968 CE
Assassination
of Dr Martin
Luther King

1969 CE
Australian
Aborigines
given the vote

1969 CE
First Moon
landing

1972 CE
Andes plane
crash

1972 CE
Death of
J. Edgar Hoover

InDEX

1990 CE
Nelson
Mandela
released
from jail

1994 CE
Nelson
Mandela
elected
President of
S. Africa

PHOTO CREDITS

2001 CE
World Trade
Center N.Y.
destroyed by
terrorists

ABOUT THE AUTHOR

Beverley MacDonald was born and raised in Victoria. Her paternal grandfather was an ANZAC at Gallipoli and France; her father was a primary school teacher in regional Victoria. After the publication of her first novel she went back to school and completed a Diploma of Professional Writing and Editing. She lives in inner Melbourne with a menagerie of people and animals.

ABOUT THE ILLUSTRATOR

Andrew Weldon's cartoons have appeared in newspapers and magazines, on greeting cards and as tattoos. They also appeared in Beverley's earlier book about the history of explosions, *Big Bangs*. Andrew has recently published his first book of cartoons, *I'm So Sorry Little Man, I Thought You Were a Hand-Puppet.*